IN AND

A DEVOTIONAL

OUT OF

MANUAL FOR THE

SEASON

MINISTER OF GOD

KENNETH KUYKENDALL

In and Out of Season
A Devotional Manual for the Minister of God
©2020 by Kenneth Kuykendall
Cross Roads Publications
ISBN: 978-0-9978232-8-8

Published by Cross Roads Publications
1391 Braselton Hwy.
Lawrenceville, GA. 30043
www.crossroadspublications.org
This cover has been designed using resources from Freepik.com by the
artist "Starline"

To the individuals who have cared for my soul, invested in my walk, and prayed for my ministry. I am eternally grateful.

Other Devotional Titles by the Author

Thrive

Pull Up a Seat

A Collection of Seasons

Somewhere in the Shadows

When God Boards Your Boat

Meditations for Ministry

The Joy of Devotion

Just Like Jesus

CONTENTS

Part 3: THE CRAFT OF THE MINISTER

Part 4: THE COMMUNION OF THE MINISTER

Part 5: THE COMPANIONS OF THE MINISTER

INTRODUCTION

Every born-again believer within a local New Testament church should consider themselves a minister of God. Too often we allot that title only to those with advanced degrees or appropriated positions. But the truth is, the word "minister" simply means "one who serves." No matter *who* you are and no matter *where* you are, you have been called by God to serve the community of faith to which you belong.

The apostle Paul said, "Therefore seeing we have this ministry, as we have received mercy, we faint not" (2 Corinthians 4:1). Say those four words to yourself: We have this ministry. Indeed, *we have* this ministry; not *they have* this ministry, not even I *have* this ministry. But we have it. It has been entrusted to every one of us.

Therefore, we must continually evaluate our hearts and minds before the Lord to secure our own spiritual strength. In every season: Whether in or out, old or new, big or small, vibrant or dry, we must be prepared to proclaim truth, care for the afflicted, and serve the body of Christ. If we fail to nourish our own souls, we will be hard-pressed to effectively minister to those around us.

This devotional manual is designed to highlight and strengthen seven key areas of ministry.

- The Minister's *Calling*
- The Minister's *Commission*
- The Minister's *Craft*
- The Minister's *Companions*
- The Minister's *Communion*
- The Minister's *Conflicts*
- The Minister's *Consolation*

No matter what stage of life or ministry you are in, I trust this book will be used as a resource to encourage you, inspire you, and equip you for the task at hand. As Paul told Timothy, "be instant in season, out of season; reprove, rebuke, exhort with all longsuffering and doctrine" As you consider the charge, may the Lord help you to "make full proof of thy ministry."

-Kenneth Kuykendall

PART 1:
THE CALLING
OF THE MINISTER

1

A SAVING CALL

Selected Reading:

Exodus 14:13, Ephesians 2:1-10, 1 Timothy 1:12-20

"Salvation is all of the grace of God.
Condemnation is all of the will of man." –Charles Spurgeon

Perhaps you have heard the story of the young boy who went forward during the invitation and prayed to receive Christ. After a few moments at the altar, the child got up and declared to the minister that he had indeed been saved. "I did my part," exclaimed the child, "and God did his part." Wanting to get some clarity about the young boy's understanding of salvation, the preacher asked, "Son, what do you mean by that?" The boy said, "Well, I did all the sinning, and God did all the saving!"

Such an answer is profoundly simple, and yet, simply profound. To be saved is the grandest reality of human existence. The fact that we "did all the sinning" suggests that we need to be saved from "all the sin." As sinners, we are transgressors of the worst lot, lawbreakers of the worst degree, blasphemers of the worst kind. Like our first parents, we have broken fellowship with God in the garden and pursued our own desires. Yes, the lust of the eyes, the lust of the flesh, and the pride of life have betrayed us. Promised to open our minds and bring life anew, they have rather destroyed our communion with the Creator and plunged us toward a payday of death. Our fig-leaf theology could not and would not cover up our iniquity. Condemned, wretched, guilty, and ashamed, we fell. We fell into an inescapable pit of miry clay. No religious maneuvering, no moral positioning, no humanistic strategizing could deliver us. We wrestle, we squirm, we try to claw our way out, but we are stuck…we are dreadfully and sinfully stuck.

But alas, the Maker of heaven and earth has reached down with a strong arm. He has condescended. He has come. He has crossed the great divide and invaded our fallenness with His own humility. He pulls us up, He pulls us out, and provides a coat of covering for our nakedness. The shame, the guilt, the iniquity, it is all gone. We have been rescued, we have been delivered, we have been saved!

John Newton said on his deathbed, "Although my memory is fading, there are two things I remember very clearly: I am a great sinner, and Christ is a great Savior." May such a memory never escape our work in the ministry. Indeed, we have done all the sinning, but God, by His marvelous and amazing grace has done all the saving. Above all else, this is the great calling of our lives.

TAKEAWAYS:

- As sinners, we have broken fellowship with God and stand eternally condemned.
- God saves us from sin and restores us through Christ.
- God calls us to be saved before He calls us to serve.

QUESTIONS:

When did you realize your need of a Savior?

_____

_____

_____

_____

_____

In your own words, describe the process of salvation.

_____

_____

_____

_____

_____

How often do share your personal testimony of salvation?

_____

_____

_____

_____

_____

PRAYER:

Dear Lord and Savior, How wonderful it is to be rescued and delivered from the bondage of my sin! Surely, I have done all the sinning, but You have done all the saving. I could not save myself, but in Your lovingkindness, You called me and brought me up with a strong arm!

2

A SOVEREIGN CALL

Selected Reading:

Genesis 12:1-9, Romans 1:1-7

"And the Lord God called unto Adam, and said unto him,
Where art thou?" –Genesis 3:9

There is a fundamental element of your calling that may seem sophomoric at first glance but it needs to be stated: You didn't call yourself. Without the approval of God's call, men are forced to manufacture their own anointing. Such ointment may cause the pulpiteer to shine for a while, but overtime it leaves a foul odor. A man without a true calling from God will work relentlessly to build his pulpit with the rarest timber, the costliest stain, and the grandest design, but he will never be able to set his Bible on it and minister from it with power and might. The call of God is not a ministerial nicety, it is a mandated necessity for the work of the kingdom.

How did Lazarus wake up from the dead after being in the grave for four days? He was called by the One Who has the voice of resurrection. Where did Moses get the courage to stand before Pharaoh and demand he let God's people go? Somewhere in the desert he stood barefooted at the burning bush and heard the Lord speak. Where did Elijah's authority come from when he climbed up Mt. Carmel and called down fire from heaven? I will tell you this, it didn't come from the school of prophets in which he was associated with; it came from the sovereign call of God in his life.

A man cannot wake himself up to this reality. He must be shaken and stirred by the voice of God. Devotional writer, Oswald Chambers said the calling of God was "baffling" and "bewildering" in the sense that it can never be fully understood or explained externally. He says that our call is rooted in the fact that "God Himself knows what He desires" and when He decides to call someone it will be His work of grace alone that initiates such an awakening.

If a man could call himself, I wonder, where would he call himself to? And what would he call himself to do? And when would he call himself to do it? The truth is, only the call of God can ignite and fuel man's destiny, direct man's path, and reveal man's purpose. And that is why you didn't, and you couldn't call yourself.

TAKEAWAYS:
- The call of God is essential for the work of the ministry.
- Man, in his own strength cannot fulfill that which only God empowers him to do.
- It is only through a divine awakening that man can come to terms with God's purpose for his life.
- We cannot call ourselves; we can only respond to God.

QUESTIONS:

What kind of awareness did you initially sense when He called you?

_____

_____

_____

_____

_____

Do you believe it is possible to reject God's call? Explain.

_____

_____

_____

_____

_____

Do you think someone can position themselves toward a calling?

_____

_____

_____

_____

_____

PRAYER:

Dear Lord, I stand amazed that You would call someone like me into the ministry. Though I feel undeserving and unworthy of such a vocation, I realize that I did not call myself. As the Potter, You have formed Your clay. Thank You for awakening in me Your holy call.

3

A SCHEDULED CALL

Selected Reading:
Ecclesiastes 3:1-15, Esther 4

"Behold, as the clay is in the potter's hand, so are
ye in mind hand, O house of Israel." –Jeremiah 18:6

When the Lord called Jeremiah the prophet, He saw fit to include some rather interesting detail. As you read through the first chapter of Jeremiah you will find some historical and cultural elements surrounding his call:

"The words of Jeremiah the son of Hilkiah, of the priests that *were* in Anathoth in the land of Benjamin: To whom the word of the LORD came in the days of Josiah the son of Amon king of Judah, in the thirteenth year of his reign. It came also in the days of Jehoiakim the son of Josiah king of Judah, unto the end of the eleventh year of Zedekiah the son of Josiah king of Judah, unto the carrying away of Jerusalem captive in the fifth month. Then the word of the LORD came unto me, saying, Before I formed thee in the belly I knew thee; and before thou camest forth out of the womb I sanctified thee, *and* I ordained thee a prophet unto the nations" (Jeremiah 1:1-5).

What seems like some rather mundane detail is really the sovereign work of God placing His minister into space, time, and history. Think about it: Geographical location, the names of political leaders, a specific time frame, relational influences, and cultural events were the surrounding elements of Jeremiah's call. At the chosen time, in the chosen place, under the chosen governmental body, with a chosen purpose, God called His chosen prophet to be a voice to His chosen nation.

Consider your own calling for just a moment and realize this glorious truth: It is a set up! God uniquely raised you up "for such a time as this." Your parents, your city, your culture, your personality, your place in history has all been divinely sanctioned by God to equip you for the task at hand.

Look at your context, look at your culture, look at your community and you will see the mighty working of God in the most miniscule of details. From the very moment you were in your mother's womb, He was setting things up for you to serve Him in your generation.

TAKEAWAYS:

- The context of our lives was designed by God to help facilitate His calling in us.
- He formed us with the intent to inform us of His will.
- Only a sovereign God can coordinate such detail.
- Before you can be a voice to the nations you must first hear the voice of the One Who is calling you.

QUESTIONS:

List some of the surrounding elements of your call:

_____

_____

_____

_____

_____

In what ways has God fashioned you in relation to your culture?

_____

_____

_____

_____

_____

List certain people or events that influenced you as a child:

_____

_____

_____

_____

_____

PRAYER:

Heavenly Father, I stand amazed when I survey all the coordinating elements of my life. You have done a work around me so that You can do a work within me. What joy thrills my heart when I consider Your ways! Thank You for this divine set up!

4

A SUSTAINED CALL

Selected Reading:

1 Kings 19:1-8, Philippians 4

"I determined never to stop until I had come to the end and achieved my purpose." –David Livingstone

The calling of God is not only the primary element of *entering* the ministry but it is also the sustaining power of *enduring* the ministry. On days of temptation, trial, and sorrow, many a minister would readily throw in the proverbial towel and move on to an easier vocation.

Think about it…Who would willingly place themselves under constant scrutiny and criticism? Who wants to schedule their lives by the calendars of other people? Who wants a phone call in the middle of the night? Who wants to miss vacation days? Who wants to bear the burdens of the bewailed? Who would eagerly offer words to dying men week after week, while realizing those very words are measured and weighed by the God of Glory? Who wants to stand at the Judgment Seat of Christ and be held accountable for the most glorious message ever given? I'll tell you who: Those who are called by God!

The calling is what sustains the minister in the most turbulent of times. Without it, your efforts will be miserable, hard-pressed, and painfully discomfited; with it, your efforts may still be those things, but the peace and assurance of God will enable you to press on with confidence that you are making a difference in the world.

The work of the ministry can exhaust you to the place of depletion. Sermons fall on deaf ears, prodigals reject the counsel, worship becomes stale, fruit becomes sparse. Like Paul of old, we say, "no man stood with me, but all men forsook me" (2 Timothy 4:16). And yet, somehow, someway, by some power, we continue and press on. Does such enablement come from innate strength? Nay, but rather we realize, "Notwithstanding the Lord stood with me and strengthened me" (2 Timothy 4:17).

Indeed, there are those out-of-season moments when all you have is the call of God upon your life. But brethren, be of good cheer, such a call is enough.

TAKEAWAYS:

- The minister's ability to persevere through difficult times is the result of God's hand upon his life.
- The true servant of the Lord looks for opportunity to help others in the time of trouble.
- Those who are called do not look for a way out during those "out of season" moments.
- The sustaining power of God will enable you to finish your course and fulfill your divine purpose.

QUESTIONS:

Can you think of a time when you felt like quitting the ministry?

_____

_____

_____

_____

_____

In what ways, specifically, has the call of God sustained you?

_____

_____

_____

_____

_____

Write out specific verses that encourage you during tough times:

_____

_____

_____

_____

_____

PRAYER:

There are times when the pressure is on, the situation is uncomfortable, and the answers are not clear. However, when I feel the weight of the ministry, somehow, I am able to press through. I know this strength does not come from myself, but rather from Your sustaining power.

5

A SUPREME CALL

Selected Reading:
Matthew 4:18-22, Mark 1:1-8, 1 Corinthians 1

"Is any man eminent in holiness and abundant in good works,
*let him take nothing of the glory to himself." –*Jonathan Edwards

D uring the days of Christ, a rabbi had many stringent requirements for his students. An impressive resume was needed just to be in consideration. The student had to have an extensive working knowledge of Scripture, be in line with the traditional Law, and live an exemplary lifestyle as required by the Sanhedrin. The application process was tedious and oftentimes the rabbi would reject those who initially applied. The student became the "identity" of the rabbi. Therefore, to safeguard his religious character and moral integrity the rabbi chose carefully and oftentimes selfishly.

When Jesus called Matthew, who sat at the seat of customs and was a hated tax collector, it must have been shocking to His colleagues. There was no entry exam, no long arduous process of inspection, no fine-tooth combing. Jesus simply said to this poor, insipid man, "Follow me." Matthew was not looking for Jesus, he submitted no application to this Rabbi, but still he was invited.

How shocking it still must be to the onlookers of the world when they see who Christ calls to follow Him. Hear the words of the apostle Paul:

> "For ye see your calling, brethren, how that not many wise men after the flesh, not many mighty, not many noble, are called: But God hath chosen the foolish things of the world to confound the wise; and God hath chosen the weak things of the world to confound the things which are mighty; And the base things of the world, and things which are despised, hath God chosen, yea, and things which are not, to bring to naught things that are:" (1 Corinthians 1:26-28).

Foolish, weak, based, despised things. That does not sound like an elite religious resume. Why does God call ordinary tax collectors, blue-collar fishermen, and common men like me and you? Here is the answer: "That no flesh should glory in his presence" (1 Corinthians 1:29). The truth is, the call of God, in and of itself, is the means by which God receives glory. If you have been called you know this to be true, let "he that glorieth, glory in the Lord."

TAKEAWAYS:

- God does not call us because we are worthy.
- His divine purpose in our life is ultimately for His glory.
- Your weakness and inability may very well be the reason God designed you for a specific area of ministry.

QUESTIONS:

How do you think the Lord is magnified through your call?

_____

_____

_____

_____

_____

Have you ever faced pride in the ministry? In what ways?

_____

_____

_____

_____

_____

How often do you consider the glory of God in your endeavors?

_____

_____

_____

_____

_____

PRAYER:

Dear Lord, it is my prayer that You would receive glory from all that is accomplished in my life. May the world see Christ in me, the hope of glory. May Your love and grace shine forth in all that You have called me to do. And may I always be found exalting You in every endeavor.

6

A STEADY CALL

Selected Reading:

Exodus 3, Jonah 2, John 21:15-25

*"What a tragedy it is in our time that we have been told to believe in him, accept him, and to seek him no more." –*A.W. Tozer

We do a great disservice to the call of God if we think of it on as an historical event. Indeed, there is a time and place when God enlightens us to the reality of His will. That is a blessed hour when the glorious light of illumination causes us to see our divine purpose in the world. However, the call of God is more than an isolated event in days gone by; it is an ever-growing, ever-expanding, ever-increasing awareness of His presence in our lives. Such an awareness affords us the opportunity to grow in our calling; or perhaps more appropriately, to have our calling grow in us.

Isaiah the prophet had been in the ministry for some time when he saw the Lord "high and lifted up." Though he had some ministerial experience and had preached several messages to the nations, God would expand his call and give him a fresh vision of Israel's true King. God opened the door of opportunity by asking,

"Who will go for us, whom shall we send?" Isaiah had been called and was still being called.

Such a statement is vitally important for the minister of God to embrace. God not only called you, He continually calls you. Your calling is not a past-tense experience documented somewhere on a theological diploma. It is living, it is breathing, it is expanding, stretching you to go beyond the comfort zone of yesterday's encounter.

Is He the God of yesterday? Yes! But He is also the God of today and the God of tomorrow! The Lord Himself said, "For he is not a God of the dead, but of the living: for all live unto him" (Luke 20:38). God called David to be a shepherd, then called him to be a giant slayer, then called him to be a king. God called Moses to be a Hebrew, then called him to be a deliverer, then He called him to be a lawgiver. God called Samuel to be a temple-worker, then a priest, then a prophet to the nations. Here's the simple truth: God calls you, and He keeps calling you until one day He calls you home!

TAKEAWAYS:

- God's call is not isolated to a one-time event.
- The Lord typically does not reveal the totality of His call in His initial work in your life.
- Over time, God will enlighten your mind and heart to His divine purpose.
- We are in a continual and perpetual state of development.

QUESTIONS:

In what ways do you sense the call of God in your life today?

_____

_____

_____

_____

_____

What do you believe is the primary task of your calling?

_____

_____

_____

_____

_____

Has God expanded your responsibilities in the ministry over time?

_____

_____

_____

_____

_____

PRAYER:

Heavenly Father, help me to hear Your call today. Give me wisdom, grace, and strength to fulfill my assignment in this moment as You continue to prepare me for the things ahead. Help me not to catalogue Your calling as an out-of-date experience but cause me to hear Your voice here and now.

7

A SPIRITUAL CALL

Selected Reading:

1 Samuel 3, John 1:43-51, 1 Peter 2:1-10

"Unbelief can render a person
stone deaf to God's voice." –Henry Blackaby

Does God still speak? I am sure you have been asked that question over the course of your ministry. The very nature of such an inquiry reveals mankind's deep and utter need to hear from God. The answer to that question is oftentimes blurred with faulty and misplaced theology. People want to hear from God, but they want to hear from God on their own terms. We want something tangible; we want something audible. We want evidence.

If we had some proof of God's voice in the physical realm, then we would readily hear what He has to say. If we could see a burning bush like Moses, if we could hear the voice of God in the temple like Samuel, if we could be given a vision like Ezekiel, then we would know, beyond any doubt that God speaks, right?

The reality is that God is Spirit, and the only way to hear the call of God is with spiritual ears. Jesus said, "He that hath ears to hear, let him hear" (Matthew 11:15). John the Revelator expressly recorded, "He that hath an ear, let him hear what the Spirit saith unto the churches" (Revelation 2:29). The writer of Hebrews said, "God, who at sundry times and in divers manners spake in time past unto the fathers by the prophets, Hath in these last days spoken unto us by his Son..." (Hebrews 1:1-2).

The work of the Spirit of God through the Word of God is far greater than an audible voice or a dramatic production. Such encounters can be manipulated, reproduced, or misinterpreted. When God speaks, He speaks in deep places. When God whispers, He whispers in the rotunda of the soul. His tone and timber are filled with glorious gravitas, rumbling down to the core of mankind.

So, the question is not whether God is speaking. He has and He does. The real question is, are we listening? Or are we so inundated with the sounds and noises of this life that we allow the menial music of the world to deafen the glorious whispers of God.

TAKEAWAYS:

- God's call cannot be reduced to the physical realm.
- He speaks through His Word, through His Spirit, and through the life and person of His Son Jesus Christ.
- If we do not hear His call it is not because He has become silent, but rather we have become distracted.
- For the minister of God to fulfill his assignment, he must stay in continual communication with the Lord.

QUESTIONS:

How would you describe the voice of God in your life?

_____

_____

_____

_____

_____

Why do you think it is so difficult for people to hear from God?

_____

_____

_____

_____

_____

Do you feel that your ministry is being guided by God's voice? How?

_____

_____

_____

_____

_____

PRAYER:

Almighty God, give me ears to hear Your voice. I admit, there are times I am easily distracted by the noise of this life. Help me to drown out the sounds of this world so that I can better experience Your presence. In Your divine instruction, give me understanding to obey your call.

8

A SACRIFICIAL CALL

Selected Reading:

Mark 6, Galatians 2:15-21, Hebrews 12:1-11

"The heart that goes out of itself
gets large and full of joy." –Horace Mann

The call of God is a gut-wrenching blow to the reality of your own dreams and plans. Bonhoeffer, in *The Cost of Discipleship,* famously said, "When Christ calls a man, He bids him come and die." One of the most paradoxical and ironic adventures in the world is to embrace the heavenly call.

You want to be first? Get to the back of the line.

You want to become great in the kingdom? Serve others.

You want to increase? Decrease.

You want to find your life? Lose it.

You want to wear a crown? Carry a cross.

If you are going to live the crucified life, you must become, of all things…crucified. I wonder if such a reality is the motivation for our ministry. "What we obtain too cheaply we esteem too little," said Thomas Pain, "it is dearness only that gives everything its value." When we give place to the call of God, we will more readily and willingly die to the things of this world. The apostle Paul said it like this:

> "But none of these things move me, neither count I my life unto myself, so that I might finish my course with joy, and the ministry, which I have received of the Lord Jesus, to testify the gospel of the grace of God" (Acts 20:24).

In the face of adversity, persecution, imprisonment, and even death, the apostle Paul found only one thing dear. It was not his life, for he had already died. What he esteemed and valued above all else was the ministry in which he had been called. Paul knew that the only way to truly walk in the power of the Spirit and fulfill his earthly assignment was to daily die to self.

If we follow the Lord, dying is not only a possibility, it is a requirement. The good news, however, is that dying does not lead to death; it leads to the divine promise of resurrection power and everlasting joy.

TAKEAWAYS:

- A man cannot follow the Lord and pursue his own dreams and aspirations at the same time.
- The call of God is a call to death.
- What we value the most is typically what we love the best.
- Although the call of God requires taking up the cross, it also produces joy in obedience, spiritual comfort, and treasures in heaven.

QUESTIONS:

In what ways do you feel you have "died" to the things of this world?

_____

_____

_____

_____

_____

Is there a "weight" or besetting sin that you wrestle with?

_____

_____

_____

_____

_____

Outside of your calling, what do you consider "dear" in your life?

_____

_____

_____

_____

_____

PRAYER:

Lord and Savior, it is easy to be driven and motivated by selfish pursuits. Even as you embraced Your cross with joy, help me to follow You with selfless passion. Give me the spirit of my calling as I follow you in this day, and every day.

9

A SPECIFIC CALL

Selected Reading:
Philippians 3:1-10, 1 Corinthians 7, 1 John 1

"We must stop setting our sights by the light of each passing ship; instead we must set our course by the stars." –George Marshall

There is nothing more miserable and displacing than when a minister of God tries to fulfill the call of someone else. The temptation to duplicate a successful ministry is an ever-present impulse of the pragmatic preacher. "Do whatever works" is the mantra of many ministers these days. The problem with such a maxim is this: What works for some may not work for others.

God may provide some men with charismatic personalities, while He fashions others to be introverts. He may send certain people to the foreign field, while He calls others to fulfill their calling locally. He creates some to be arms, some to be feet, and others to be ears. It is His Body. It is His prerogative. It is His business. Our business is to accept His call and serve accordingly.

Philips Brooks said, "Get the pattern of your life from God, then go about your work and be yourself." This is the same counsel the apostle Paul gave the Corinthian believers. In response to their prideful and inner squabbling, Paul said:

> "Let every man abide in the same calling wherein he was called. Art thou called *being* a servant? care not for it: but if thou mayest be made free, use *it* rather. For he that is called in the Lord, *being* a servant, is the Lord's freeman: likewise also he that is called, *being* free, is Christ's servant. Ye are bought with a price; be not ye the servants of men. Brethren, let every man, wherein he is called, therein abide with God" (1 Corinthians 7:20-24).

Not once, but twice in this passage Paul admonished them to "abide in their calling." There is nothing wrong with having spiritual heroes. There is nothing inherently sinful about studying other men's methods and procedures. However, when we try to abide in a calling that was not designed for our lives, it will be oddly detected by others. Worse still, we will miss out on the joy and pleasure of fulfilling our God-given purpose. Abide in your calling and the promise is this: God will abide with you.

TAKEAWAYS:

- Pragmatism is a dangerous way to approach ministry.
- God's calling is uniquely fashioned and detailed for the individual that He calls.
- Being something that God has not equipped you to be leads to a pretentious and unfruitful ministry.
- The greatest joy you will have in the ministry is to grow where God plants you.

QUESTIONS:

Do you allow external influences to control the desires of your heart?

_____

_____

_____

_____

_____

In your own words, what does it mean to "abide in your calling?"

_____

_____

_____

_____

_____

Have you ever tried to duplicate someone else's success? Explain.

_____

_____

_____

_____

_____

PRAYER:

Heavenly Father, I am guilty of comparing my ministry with the work of others. Rid my heart of envy, criticism, or covetousness. May I learn to abide in my calling with peace and joy. Produce fruit in my labor and help me to serve you gladly where I have been planted.

10

A SUPERNATURAL CALL

Selected Reading:

Romans 8:18-39, 2 Corinthians 4, Revelation 21

"What a father says to his son is not heard by the world...
but it will be heard in posterity." –Jean Paul Richter

The very moment Paul was knocked off his beast by the Lord on the Damascus Road, his life would never be the same. Chosen by God to be a vessel of light to the Gentiles, Paul would radically influence the circles of Judaism and Christianity by revealing the great mysteries of God concerning His church. The zealous animosity he possessed against Christ and His disciples would be reallocated by God's grace to help propagate the gospel and grow the church to regions beyond Jerusalem.

For Paul, there was no turning back, there was no place of rest, there was not point of return. The heavenly call consumed his life with such intensity that he likened it unto a race. He said,

"Brethren, I count not myself to have apprehended: but *this* one thing *I do*, forgetting those things which are behind, and reaching forth unto those things which are before,

I press toward the mark for the prize of the high calling of God in Christ Jesus. Let us therefore, as many as be perfect, be thus minded: and if in any thing ye be otherwise minded, God shall reveal even this unto you" (Philippians 3:13-15).

Paul was running after something that had its abode in another world. Like an Olympian who focused his attention and efforts toward the finish line, Paul knew there was a reward waiting at the end. In his final words to Timothy he talked about the "crown of righteousness, which the Lord, the righteous judge" should give to him on that day.

By the calculations of the world, it may seem as though your calling has little-to-no value. Oftentimes we feel like no-name servants working in no-name locations with no-name ministries. But the truth is, the prize of our calling is waiting. A crown of righteousness is prepared. The triumph of heaven is our destination, and the ultimate reward is that we will one day see face to face the One who has been with us every step of the journey. On that day, our heavenly call will be validated by a heavenly reward!

TAKEAWAYS:

- If you have been called, there is no quitting place.
- God has promised a reward for those who finish their race.
- The world may never value your calling, but remember, what you are doing is not for the world, it is for Christ.
- The final state of the call of God is to be with the Lord forever in heaven.

QUESTIONS:

In what ways do you feel God has blessed your calling?

_____

_____

_____

_____

_____

What do you think Paul meant by the "prize of the high calling?"

_____

_____

_____

_____

_____

What hinderances do you readily experience in your race?

_____

_____

_____

_____

_____

PRAYER:

Dear Lord, it is with great joy I press toward the mark for the prize of the high calling. Like Paul, I realize that I am not all that I am supposed to be, but one day, I will be like You. And that is the ultimate prize of the calling, to be with You in heaven forever. I am glad you will finish Your work in me on that day.

PART 2:
THE COMMISSION
OF THE MINISTER

11

AS A PREACHER

Selected Reading:

Acts 5:42, Colossians 1:28, Titus 1:1-3

"I preached as never sure to be preaching again,
*and as a dying man to dying me." –*Richard Baxter

Though Bible preaching is considered an antiquated notion in this post-modern world, the act of heralding God's Word is still the divine design whereby truth is illuminated and revealed to the hearers. Preaching is at the core of New Testament Christianity. Without it, you cannot evangelize the world, equip the church, overcome the enemy, comprehend the mysteries, facilitate worship, or have a clear understanding of the Person and work of Christ. The mandate is clearly articulated in Scripture: We are to preach the Word!

God works through the "foolishness of preaching" to make His truth known to humanity. Perhaps Paul said it most clearly when he declared that God has "manifested his word through preaching" (Titus 1:3). In its most basic and biblical definition, "preaching" is simply the act of proclaiming, heralding, and propagating God's Word in an audible and public way especially as it relates to the gospel of Jesus Christ. Corresponding with this endeavor is the idea of explaining, reasoning, and teaching others the truth of Scripture. Therefore, the act of preaching is inseparable from the Word of God. Biblical preaching cannot take place outside the realm of divine revelation. Where there is no Scripture being explained, there is no authority being given, which means there are no lives being changed. Such a tragedy is ever-present in our world. The apostle Paul said:

> "For the time will come when they will not endure sound doctrine; but after their own lusts shall they heap to themselves teachers, having itching ears; And they shall turn away their ears from the truth, and shall be turned to fables" (2 Timothy 3:3-4).

Regardless of what is happening in our culture, we are to "Preach the word; be instant in season, out of season; reprove, rebuke, exhort with all longsuffering and doctrine" (2 Timothy 3:2). We are not called to preach our opinions, our thoughts, or even our outlines. Rather, we have been commissioned to go into the world and preach the gospel of Jesus Christ, for it is the power of God unto salvation. May we say with the apostle Paul, "So, as much as in me is, I am ready to **preach** the gospel!"

TAKEAWAYS:

- God chooses preaching as the means to present His truth.
- Preaching is the act of heralding the gospel and Scripture.
- It is the Word, not opinions, that will transform lives.

QUESTIONS:

Explain the term "the foolishness of preaching."

_____

_____

_____

_____

_____

Explain how preaching is dependent upon God's Word.

_____

_____

_____

_____

_____

What challenges exist for the preacher in these days?

_____

_____

_____

_____

_____

PRAYER:

Dear Lord, Woe unto me if I preach not the gospel! Let me not only proclaim the Good News but help me to live by it as well. Consecrate my heart, illuminate my mind, and anoint my lips to declare the glorious truth of Thy Word. Help me to be instant in season and out of season.

12

AS A PASTOR

Selected Reading:
Jeremiah 10:21, Ephesians 4:11, 1 Timothy 3:1-7

"And I will give you pastors according to mine heart, which shall feed you with knowledge and understanding." –Jeremiah 3:15

To desire the vocation of a pastor is to desire a good work (1 Timothy 3:10). Contrary to popular belief, the "work of a bishop" extends far beyond the hour of exposition. Some contend the "only thing" a pastor does is preach thirty minutes a week for worship services. If preaching were the "only thing" the pastor did, that alone would occupy countless hours of study, prayer, and preparation. The truth is the pastor does not just lead God's people by preaching to them; he is required by God to live in righteousness before the flock.

The pastor must be an example to God's people. Paul said the bishop must be "blameless," or quite literally, one who cannot be legally charged in a court of law. Therefore, the moral character of the pastor is always on display. Everything from his family, to his work ethic, to his financial decisions abide in the proverbial glass house of his life. It is from this position he is to lead the flock.

The pastor must love and care for God's people. Pastors may have great intellect, personality, and charm; but if they do not genuinely care for their flock, as Christ cared for His sheep, they are nothing more than hirelings serving their own selfish purpose.

The pastor must feed and nourish God's people. The Word of God is the premium diet for every flock. A good shepherd knows his sheep individually and understands how to feed them based upon their spiritual maturity. He must "feed the flock of God which is among you, taking the oversight thereof." (1 Peter 5:2). Word by word, line by line, precept by precept, the shepherd is required to faithfully teach and preach truth.

The pastor must rebuke and correct God's people. As difficult as it may be, the shepherd is scripturally obligated to "reprove, rebuke, and exhort with all longsuffering and doctrine" (2 Timothy 4:2). A true shepherd will care enough for God's flock to go after every wandering sheep. Though painful for a season, the work of restoration brings gladness and strength to the fold.

The pastor must follow the Chief Shepherd. Pastoral ministry is a continual labor of love. There is rarely a moment when the flock is without need or want. To secure the strength and spiritual stability of his own soul, the pastor must stay close to the Chief Shepherd. To this end, the "good work" is sure to be maintained.

TAKEAWAYS:

- The "good work" of a pastor has biblical requirements.
- Though preaching is fundamental, it is not the only task.
- The pastor ministers from his moral and spiritual integrity.

QUESTIONS:

List any other attributes and responsibilities of the pastorate.

_____

_____

_____

_____

_____

How does living in a "glass house" effect your family?

_____

_____

_____

_____

_____

How does following the Good shepherd empower your leadership?

_____

_____

_____

_____

_____

PRAYER:

Almighty God, You are the Shepherd and the Bishop of my soul. As I consider this awesome responsibility of leading Your flock, help me to stay close to Your side. Lead me as I lead others. Guide me as I guide Your people. Help me to live before them as an example of righteousness.

13

AS A TEACHER

Selected Reading:
2 Samuel 1:18, Ezra 7:10-25, Psalm 143:10

"It was my teacher's genius, her quick sympathy, her loving tact,
which made the first years of my education so beautiful." –Helen Keller

C losely associated with the office of the bishop is the role
and responsibility of the Bible teacher. Not all teachers
are pastors, but all pastors are scripturally required to be
teachers. When describing the various leadership positions in the
church, the apostle Paul said:

> "And God hath set some in the church, first apostles,
> secondarily prophets, thirdly *teachers*...after that miracles,
> then gifts of healings, helps, governments, diversities of
> tongues" (1 Corinthians 12:28)

> "And he gave some, apostles; and some, prophets; and some,
> evangelists; and some, pastors and *teachers*;" (Ephesians 4:11)

The pastor/teacher relationship is so congruently linked that many
believe Paul used the two words interchangeably to describe the
work of the bishop. This clearly demonstrates how weighty and
significant the work of teaching is to the body of Christ. Teaching,

in its most simplistic definition can be described as the ability to instruct and impart knowledge. The Bible teacher who can clearly explain the profound mysteries of the Word is uniquely positioned to equip and empower God's people for righteous living.

Consider the ministry of Apollos. Working closely with the apostle Paul, he was known to be "an eloquent man, and mighty in the Scriptures…(who) taught diligently the things of the Lord" (Acts 18:24-25). His teaching ministry at Corinth and Ephesus had a profound impact on the congregation. Paul said, "I have planted, Apollos watered; but God gave the increase" (1 Corinthians 3:6). His teaching ministry helped grow and nurture the gospel seeds of the apostle Paul to a harvest of souls.

Like Apollos, Bible teachers should be considered "gifts" to the body of Christ as they help educate and equip the saints for ministry (Ephesians 4:12). Teachers facilitate knowledge. They answer questions. They make application. They clearly illustrate. They inspire. They take that which is difficult and make it easily understood. They embody the characteristics of Christ, Who Himself was "a teacher come from God" (John 3:2).

Whether you teach a small class of middle-school students or a large auditorium of senior saints, embrace the awesome task set before you. Prepare the lesson; class is in session.

TAKEAWAYS:

- Teachers have the unique gift of explaining God's Word.
- The work of the teacher is to equip the saints of God.
- The Bible teacher is positioned to help nurture the gospel.

QUESTIONS:

Regardless of position, how does teaching fit into your ministry?

_____

_____

_____

_____

_____

What are some unique qualities of an effective Bible teacher?

_____

_____

_____

_____

_____

How does the Bible teacher equip the saints for the ministry?

_____

_____

_____

_____

_____

PRAYER:

Holy Savior, I thank You for the various teachers You have given me in my life. Their influence has had a tremendous effect on my spiritual growth. Help me to teach others also and equip the saints for the work of the ministry. Whether I plant or water, may You give the increase!

14

AS AN EVANGELIST

Selected Reading:

Luke 10:1-12, Acts 21:8, 2 Timothy 4:5

"God forbid that I should travel with anybody a quarter of an hour without speaking of Christ to them." –George Whitefield

I have fond memories of church revivals from my youth. My pastor, who was also my grandfather, would invite guest preachers to come for a week at a time and fill the pulpit. I remember the excitement that came along with those meetings and those men. They were fresh voices with interesting stories, powerful delivery styles, and strong personalities. Weeks before the meeting, you would see "flyers" posted on the Sunday school bulletin board reminding everyone of the evangelist who would be preaching. Each night before they preached, the introduction of "evangelist" always accompanied their names.

I am thankful for the work of such men. Through the years, they have spiritually fed my soul and encouraged my faith. They travel, they preach, they pray, they exhort, they rebuke, they help fan the flame of revival. They too, along with pastors and teachers, have been given to the church as a measure of grace.

It should be clarified, however, that an evangelist is not just one who comes into town and preaches a series of church services. Though such a task is part of their calling, the primary responsibility of the evangelist is to "go forth and proclaim the good news of Jesus Christ." The Greek word is *euaggelistes* which specifically refers to those who herald the gospel in various places.

Paul told Timothy, who was the pastor at Ephesus, to "do the work of an evangelist, make full proof of thy ministry" (2 Timothy 4:5). Did this mean that Timothy should leave the pastorate and pursue a full-time vocation as an itinerant preacher? No, it simply meant that Timothy was supposed to share the gospel wherever he went. He was to fulfill the Great Commission as a disciple.

We do a disservice to the role of the evangelist when we reduce his obligations only to be fulfilled in a church service. The evangelistic heart is one that beats inside *and* outside the church walls. He is one that spreads the gospel near and far, here and there. Though his calendar book may be filled with scheduled meetings and revivals, he understands that his work of heralding the gospel goes beyond the church meeting. His identity is not legitimized through a flyer or an advertisement. He goes forth and shares the gospel everywhere simply because he has been called.

TAKEAWAYS:

- The biblical evangelist is a gift to the body of Christ.
- The evangelist is one who is called to spread the gospel of Jesus Christ in various places.
- Evangelism cannot be reduced to a schedule of meetings.

QUESTIONS:

In your opinion, what is the primary responsibility of the evangelist?

_____

_____

_____

_____

_____

In what ways do you function as an evangelist?

_____

_____

_____

_____

_____

Do you agree with this assessment of the evangelist? Explain.

_____

_____

_____

_____

_____

PRAYER:

Great and Almighty God, I thank You for the men You have called and gifted to do the work of evangelism. I pray You will fill them with Your Spirit and power. Help them as they labor in the harvest fields. Help me to join them in their endeavors to spread the gospel of Jesus Christ.

15

AS A SERVANT

Selected Reading:
John 13:1-20, Philippians 2:5-11, James 4:6-10

*"You can have no greater sign of confirmed pride than
when you think you are humble enough."* –William Law

The unhealthy and never-ending hunger for approval is one of the hallmarks of our generation. Such a religious pursuit is not new; even the closest companions of Christ wrestled with ego, "Then there arose a reasoning among them, which of them should be greatest" (Luke 9:46).

The "reasoning" process among the disciples was a self-absorbed, narcissistic competition that gave no thought of the glory of Christ. For had Christ been factored into their reasoning, there would have been no discussion nor debate; Jesus is the greatest, the most magnanimous of all-time. And yet Christ bowed divine knees and made this radical statement to those glory-hungry disciples, "I am among you as he that serveth" (Luke 22:27).

I say "radical" because the concept of being a servant doesn't seemingly match the glorious nature of Christ's person. Christ is King, Master, Messiah, God incarnate; yet He sought to be servant among sinners. The word "serveth" is *diakoneo* in the Greek, which comes from *diakonos*. This word is translated as "minister, ministering, service, servant, and even deacon." The word literally means, "kicking up dust, or walking through the dust."

The genesis of the word stems from the camel-trade days. Whenever a master would purchase a camel, the servant would hoist his master onto the beast and literally "walk through the dust" as he led the animal to the desired location. The servant was abased so the master could be exalted.

When Christ said, "I am among you as he that serveth," He was literally saying, "I will take the lowest position, I am willing to be inconvenienced and walk through the dust for each of you." This is true greatness, at least the kind that is recognized by God.

Men and women who influence the kingdom are those who serve others as Christ served His disciples. They help others reach their potential. They set others on the beast. They wash feet. They clean toilets. They whisper prayers. They do all these things without need for applause. Their hands are calloused, their hearts are tender, their minds are lowly, their desires are pure, and their feet are dusty. They serve others...because they are like Christ.

TAKEAWAYS:

- Pride and self-glory are constant temptations for mankind.
- True greatness in the kingdom is to serve others with a spirit of humility.
- If Christ "walked through the dust" for His disciples, we should be willing to wash the feet of those around us.

QUESTIONS:

In all honesty, do you view yourself as a servant? Why or why not?

_____

_____

_____

_____

_____

Give examples of Christ's demonstration of service to others.

_____

_____

_____

_____

_____

List specific ways in which you can serve others around you.

_____

_____

_____

_____

_____

PRAYER:

Great Omnipotent God, I stand amazed that You would humble Yourself and take upon the form of a servant. Such a thought convicts my heart to assume the position of humility and serve others. Guard my heart from pride and self-glory and help me "walk through the dust" for You.

16

AS AN AMBASSADOR

Selected Reading:
Proverbs 13:7, Jeremiah 49:14, Obadiah 1:1

"Some wish to live within the sound of a chapel bell, I wish to run a rescue mission within a yard of hell." –C.T. Studd

Pollsmoor Prison was one of the most violent and deadliest institutions in South Africa in the late 1990's. It was known for gang warfare, daily bloodshed, a corrupt administration, and political unrest. Through the years, aggressive conflict resolution initiatives had been implemented to resolve the turmoil that existed at Pollsmoor, but to no avail. The spiritual darkness on campus was strong; it needed a light from another world. Enter Joanna Thomas.

Knowing the spiritual strongholds in the prison, Joanna and her husband began visiting the prison every day, praying fervently for souls. They were granted permission to start bible studies, chapel services, and discipleship programs. Persistently, they engaged the prisoners with the love of God and the gospel of Jesus Christ. It did not take long for the light to penetrate the dark hearts of Pollsmoor. The behavioral climate began to change in such a dramatic way, that documentary teams wanted to interview the couple to uncover their secret. Years of psychology, politics, money, incarceration, and law enforcement could not change the cultural landscape of the prison; the gospel changed it with a few months. In an interview, they were asked how "the God-forsaken" prison had been changed. Joanna replied, "God was already here, we just had to make Him known."

Such is the response and the mindset of an ambassador.

Paul said of himself, "For which I am an ambassador in bonds: that therein I may speak boldly, as I ought to speak" (Ephesians 6:20). Furthermore, he said of all believers, "Now then we are ambassadors for Christ, as though God did beseech *you* by us: we pray *you* in Christ's stead, be ye reconciled to God" (2 Corinthians 5:20).

An ambassador is a spiritual diplomat who is authorized to speak as God's emissary. He is a sanctioned statesman, a divine delegate who operates on behalf of another kingdom. As ambassadors for God, we have the monumental task of making Christ and His rule of law known throughout the world. As we shine His gospel light and spread His gospel truth, we can see the most hellish of prisons turn into the holiest of cathedrals.

TAKEAWAYS:

- Being an ambassador means being Christ's representative.
- God chooses to make Himself know through the life and ministry of His people.
- We must safeguard our testimony as to not be a reproach.

QUESTIONS:

Do you believe all Christians are ambassadors? Why or why not?

_____

_____

_____

_____

_____

How does being an ambassador specifically impact your ministry?

_____

_____

_____

_____

_____

What kind of relationship do you have with your community?

_____

_____

_____

_____

_____

PRAYER:

Dear Lord and Savior, as Your representative, as Your ambassador, help me to be pleasing and acceptable in Your sight. May I live my life in such a way that I am never a reproach to Your kingdom. Help me shine Your light in this dark and evil world so that men will know You. Amen.

17

AS A SOLDIER

Selected Reading:

2 Chronicles 25, Luke 7:8, Philemon 1:2

"Soon the battle will be over…and our Commander will call us away from the battlefield for the victor's crown." –Thomas Watson

The modern minister wears a lot of different hats these days. Contemporary church culture wants the clergymen to be well versed in every facet of life. He is to be a speaker, a coach, a counselor, a visionary, an administrator, a social advocate, a scholar, a consultant, an entertainer, and the list goes on and on. Bill Hull, in his discipleship book, *Choose the Life*, said of today's minister:

> "Culture tells us we are to be really nice people who open the Little League season with a prayer or say a benediction at the dedication of a new building site. Culture wants us to pepper their lives with a little moral trust to get them through hard times. They really just want us to be chaplains, to marry, bury, and perform all the duties of our society."

Out of all the hats society wants the man of God to wear, I suppose a helmet is not typically one of them. A helmet, though, is what God requires in the service of the Lord. If we reduce our ministries to mere social niceties, we are nothing more than motivational speakers who will inevitably flee the religious scene during the pressures of wartime.

Soldiers…that is what we are. Rejection of such a title not only puts the minister of God at risk, but equally endangers all those around him. At some point the soldier must draw his sword from the sheath while drawing his line in the sand. He must gird up the loins of his mind, put on the whole armor of God and stand ready to defend his territory.

He does not make decisions based upon cultural trends, opinion polls, or contemporary persuasion. Rather, he receives his orders from the Captain. He stands at the attention of the Lord. He hears His call and obeys His command. Though he does not want to die in battle, he is prepared to lay down his life for the King and His kingdom if need be.

The soldier of Jesus Christ can at times seem brazen, offensive, and culturally off-putting; yet without him, the church stands vulnerable to ongoing attack. To this end, Paul said, "Fight the good fight of faith, lay hold on eternal life, whereunto thou art called, and has professed a good profession before many witnesses" (1 Timothy 6:12). Onward Christian soldier!

TAKEAWAYS:

- The identity of the minister is one of a solider in combat.
- The fight of faith requires allegiance to the Captain alone.
- The last days will bring about opposition to the minister.

QUESTIONS:

What attributes of your ministry come off as a soldier?

_____

_____

_____

_____

_____

What do you think the greatest battles are in the church?

_____

_____

_____

_____

_____

In what areas of your ministry do you sense the most opposition?

_____

_____

_____

_____

_____

PRAYER:

Dear Lord, as my Commanding Officer, help me to fight the good fight of faith. At times the battle rages, the enemy is strong, and the fight becomes difficult. Help me to draw my sword, nonetheless, and stand for the truth of Your Word. As Your soldier, give me victory in Your name.

18

AS A THEOLOGIAN

Selected Reading:
Nehemiah 8, Luke 24:27, 2 Timothy 2:15

"No man that has not the vitals for theology is capable of going beyond a fool in philosophy." –Richard Baxter

The concept of the minister being a theologian may initially be taken as an academic thought, one that promotes advanced degrees, seminary training, and scholarly pursuits. Such realities may be part of the preacher's development, but the true theologian needs no cap and gown for God's approval.

Indeed, God has chosen "weak things" to confound the strong, and "foolish things" to confound the wise. Paul said, "For ye see your calling, brethren, how that not many wise men after the flesh, not many mighty, not many noble, are called" (1 Corinthians 1:26). However, God's sovereign act of calling His chosen vessels does not absolve man of ignorance. Solomon said:

> Get wisdom, get understanding: forget *it* not; neither decline from the words of my mouth. Forsake her not, and she shall preserve thee: love her, and she shall keep thee. Wisdom *is* the

principal thing; *therefore* get wisdom: and with all thy getting get understanding" (Proverbs 4:5-7).

The church has a rich history of men who had no formal training but were theologians, nonetheless. Men like John Bunyan, Charles Spurgeon, and Martyn Lloyd-Jones pursued "the principal thing" and with all their "getting" they "got understanding."

This must be our pursuit as theologians. We are to study, learn, and teach sound doctrine. We systematically build our faith upon theological truths that can only be discovered in Scripture. We examine and contemplate the deep-rooted issues of mankind and resolve such matters with biblical knowledge. With the tone of an apologist, we earnestly defend and contend for Scripture.

"If you do not listen to theology," said C.S Lewis, "that will not mean you have no ideas about God, rather it will mean you have a lot of wrong ones." We are called to impart the right ideas of God to His people. When the minister becomes a theologian, faith is strengthened in the congregation through the power of the Word. Revival, therefore, is made possible in the lives of God's people because they have been adequately exposed to the truth. The minister may never walk across the stage to receive a degree, but if he is called by God, his thirst for theology will keep him in the classroom all the days of his life.

TAKEAWAYS:

- Being a theologian doesn't require an advanced degree.
- At the heart of theology is the desire for sound doctrine.
- People will never live out what they do not know.

QUESTIONS:

How has your theological understanding been developed?

_____

_____

_____

_____

_____

Is formal training and education necessary for ministry?

_____

_____

_____

_____

_____

How does theology fit into the narrative of your ministerial work?

_____

_____

_____

_____

_____

PRAYER:

Word of God, I pray that You would speak to me through the Scriptures. Help me to embrace, study, and proclaim sound doctrine to Your people. Thank you for the desire of knowledge. Help me to solidify what I believe through the ongoing study of Your Word.

19

AS A DISCIPLE-MAKER

Selected Reading:

Matthew 24:3, Luke 6:40, Acts 9:10-19

"Discipleship is a daily discipline. We follow Jesus one step at a time, one day at a time." –Warren Wiersbe

The only way New Testament Christianity can multiply and function in the world is if disciples of Jesus Christ make disciple-makers within the church. Discipleship is not filling the church up with people, nor is about filling the people up with church; it is about equipping believers with truth so they can be conformed to the image of Christ. It is only when those individuals begin repeating the process that true discipleship takes place.

This scriptural mandate of discipleship far exceeds a course or program; rather it is a lifelong conformity to Jesus. God has not called us to grow His church, He alone does that; instead, He has called us to grow disciples, and when we grow disciples, He will inevitably build His church. So, the real question is not "are we making disciples?" but rather, "are we making disciples who are disciple-makers?"

Paul said, "And the things which thou hast heard of me among many witnesses, the same commit thou to faithful men, who shall be able to teach others also" (2 Timothy 2:2). This intentional plan of discipleship was tiered in such a way to facilitate truth far beyond individual soul winning. Consider this:

- Paul was a disciple-maker.
- Paul taught Timothy to be a disciple-maker.
- Timothy taught faithful men to be disciple-makers.
- Faithful men taught others whom we would assume were disciple-makers.

When individuals are taught biblical truth within the framework of an accountable discipling relationship, spiritual growth and stability takes root in the heart of the church. Oswald Sanders said,

> It (discipleship) requires patient, careful instruction and prayerful, personal guidance over a considerable amount of time. Disciples are not manufactured wholesale. They are reproduced, only one by one, because someone has taken the pains to instruct, enlighten, nurture and train them."

God's ministers must initiate the call, engage the work, and take the first steps to provide a community of discipleship. This happens when the minister of God is a disciple-maker himself.

TAKEAWAYS:

- We reproduce what we are, not just what we know.
- Disciples are called to make disciple-makers.
- Such an endeavor takes patience, truth, and fellowship.

QUESTIONS:

What is the biblical definition of a disciple?

_____

_____

_____

_____

_____

Why should we make disciple-makers and not just disciples?

_____

_____

_____

_____

_____

List key individuals in your life who have taught you biblical truth.

_____

_____

_____

_____

_____

PRAYER:

Great and Holy God, how wonderful it is to be in a community of faith. Thank You for the people in my life who have invested in my relationship with You. Help me to instruct and lead others into a meaningful, growing walk with the Savior. Help them to do the same with others.

20

AS A WORSHIPPER

Selected Reading:
Deuteronomy 26:10, Psalm 86, Luke 17:11-19

*"For ten thousand unobserved or unremembered mercies,
let us unweariedly bless His holy name."* –David McIntyre

Neglect of worship makes bare the heart and soul of the minister. One can cross every theological "t," and dot every expositional "i" and still be as hollow as the heretic, as pitiful as the pagan. The "letter" of the law may clothe the most pious man with the finest religious garb, but it does so with the intent to kill. There is not a more distressing oxymoron in the body of Christ than the minister who has lost his thrill of worship and praise.

Imagine such a thing: A "worshipless" worship leader.

What a strange occurrence it is that a minister who has been called to lead others in praise has little of it in his heart. Like Asaph of old, who led Israel's worship in the golden era of David, we too can "lose our song in the night" and experience the dry, cold, despondent mechanics of worship. It is imperative that the minister guard his heart against such indifference. But how?

Through gratitude. Paul said, "Rejoice evermore. Pray without ceasing. In everything give thanks for this is the will of God in Christ Jesus concerning you" (2 Thessalonians 5:16-18). Nothing ignites the heart of praise like expressing our appreciate to God for all His daily benefits. If you want to be in His will, worship.

Through obedience. Without compliance to His Word, worship cannot take place. Jesus said, "If ye love me, keep my commandments" (John 14:15). Those who please the Lord in obedience, will be pleased by the Lord in worship.

Through holiness. Only those with clean hands and pure hearts can ascend to the holy hill. Worship is non-existent in the lives of unholy people. Tozer said, "There is no worship wholly pleasing to God till there is nothing in us displeasing to God."

Through the Spirit. God is Spirit and they that worship Him must worship Him in spirit and truth. Yes, the "letter killeth" but the Spirit gives us life...a life of worship. Apart from the quickening power of the Spirit, true worship cannot exist.

Through service. Service cannot be a substitute for worship. If it is, we are no better than Martha who opted out of "the good part" in exchange for her meal prep. But when we view our serve as an act of worship, then what we do, no matter what it is, becomes a symphony of praise.

TAKEAWAYS:

- Leaders are vulnerable to become cold in their worship.
- Ministry and service are not substitutes for praise.
- The minister must be proactive in keeping his heart pure.

QUESTIONS:

Can you describe a time when you were disconnected in worship?

_____

_____

_____

_____

_____

As a worship leader, what do you do to keep your heart in tune?

_____

_____

_____

_____

_____

How does the Spirit of God enable us to worship?

_____

_____

_____

_____

_____

PRAYER:

Holy Savior, I bless Your name at all times. Whether it is in the privacy of my closet or in the public setting of the sanctuary, I praise You and glorify You. May Your Spirit be pleased with my worship and may I humble my heart before You. With a voice of thanksgiving I offer praise.

PART 3:
THE CRAFT
OF THE MINISTER

PREPARATION

Selected Reading:
1 Chronicles 15:1-12, Amos 4:12, Galatians 1:15-24

*"When opportunity comes, it is
too late to prepare."* –John Wooden

When God calls a man to the service of the Lord, He is calling that man to a life of preparation. Ministry is essentially a sequence of days in which the man of God faithfully does his homework and heart-work together. The influence he may have while in front of his class, his congregation, or his community is only made possible by the personal and private hours he spends preparing himself for the opportunity.

Consider the ministry of the apostle Paul. Shortly after his calling, the Lord directed him toward Arabia where he spent nearly three years preparing for the gospel ministry. I am not suggesting that Paul did nothing during those years, but it is evident the Lord used that private season of Paul's life to reveal the great mysteries of the church. In the shadows of preparation, God did a work that would eventually be brought to light throughout the entire world. Such is the pattern of God's working in us. God provides us with an opportunity to prepare, so that when we faithfully prepare, we will be given an opportunity to serve. So, the question is: How does a minister of the Lord make preparation for his ministerial obligations?

Through Devotion. The minister must maintain communion with the Lord if he wants to be effective in public ministry. He must not view himself as a mere employee of the kingdom, but rather as a son in relationship with the Father. His hours of preparation must reflect that spiritual reality.

Through Discipline. No one typically knows or sees the private moments of the minister. Therefore, it is imperative that he uses his time wisely. He must avoid distraction and interruptions at all cost. Apathy and laziness have no place in God's work.

Through Discernment. During the hours of preparation, the minister of God is considering all things spiritual. He must seek the mind of God, he must consider the spiritual condition of his people, he must think, pray, write, read, process, and pursue truth, later to be communicated to those he serves.

Through Development. Preparation not only develops the man of God; it allows the man of God to develop what he is to do in his hour of opportunity. The best chance to succeed at tomorrow's assignment is to take advantage of the preparatory work today.

TAKEAWAYS:

- A call to ministry is a call to prepare.
- Public opportunities are qualified by private preparation.
- *Repairing* is more challenging than *preparing*.

QUESTIONS:

How much time per week do you put into ministry preparation?

_____

_____

_____

_____

_____

What are the biggest hinderances you face during prep time?

_____

_____

_____

_____

_____

Do you have a developed routine for your study? If so, describe:

_____

_____

_____

_____

_____

PRAYER:

Holy God, Allow me to see the importance of preparation. Help me to come into that designated hour with a clear mind, a ready heart, and a willing spirit to receive Your truth, guidance, and will for myself and those I serve. Keep me from distractions and help me to commune with You above all else. Amen.

22

SUPPLICATION

Selected Reading:
Genesis 32, Habakkuk 3, John 18:1-11

*"If I wished to humble anyone, I would
ask him about his prayers."* –C.J. Vaughan

When it comes to the matter of prayer, I feel
somewhat like D. Martyn Lloyd-Jones did in
describing the "diffidence, hesitation, and utter
unworthiness" in tackling the subject. Fearful of making prayer a
mechanical exercise, Jones was reluctant to write a book or
booklet on the topic, believing too many writers approached
prayer with a sophomoric classification of do's and don'ts. "It all
seems so simple," said Jones, "but prayer is not simple." I concur;
of all the spiritual activities in which a minister is expected to
embrace, prayer, at least in my own experience, is perhaps the
most perplexing and easily neglected.

Possibly, the original twelve felt the same way. When the
disciples sought to improve their own prayer lives, they did not
ask Jesus *how* to pray, but rather succinctly, "Lord, teach us *to*
pray" (Luke 11:1). The real issue is not the mechanics of prayer,

but rather the motivation. If we are not careful, we can become so preoccupied with "how to pray" that we lose the wonder, intimacy, and purpose of the actual act of praying. It is reasonable to conclude the only way to improve your prayer life is to develop the discipline to pray. In the classic volume, *Shepherding God's Flock*, Jay Adams contends:

> "In this one word (prayer), the simplest, yet probably the most difficult part of the pastoral work is identified. The real difficulty for the pastor is to pray well. He must recognize that prayer is not merely a personal matter but is a part of the pastoral task to which he has been called. Prayer, then, is work, work that in order to do well he must take the time to do and for which he must develop the self-discipline."

Jones and Adams both agreed that prayer is a difficult endeavor; one that requires time, discipline, and perhaps most problematic, honesty. Nevertheless, without prayer, the minister of God will be hard-pressed and ill-suited for any spiritual exercise. For it is through the spiritual exercise of prayer that all other spiritual exercises are fueled. No matter what field of service you are in, the prayer closet awaits. As Oswald Chambers said, "Prayer does not fit us for the greater work, prayer is the greater work."

TAKEAWAYS:

- Prayer can be the grandest struggle of the minister.
- A desire for God is the true catalyst for praying.
- Prayer is the fuel for all other ministry endeavors.

QUESTIONS:

How much of your ministry would still operate if you did not pray?

_____

_____

_____

_____

_____

What are the biggest challenges you encounter in prayer?

_____

_____

_____

_____

_____

Describe any answers to prayer you have recently experienced.

_____

_____

_____

_____

_____

PRAYER:

Dear Lord and Savior, I pray as the disciples prayed...teach me to pray. Not just the mechanics, or the motions, or the memorization of prayer, but create in me a desire to want to pray. Many times, I struggle with making my way to the prayer closet. Give me a hunger to know You in prayer. Let prayer be the catalyst for all I do in the ministry.

23

EXAMINATION

Selected Reading:
Jeremiah 20:1-9, Psalm 119:1-16, 2 Peter 1:16-21

"We must not only lay it (the Bible) up within us, but transfuse it through the whole texture of the soul." –Horatius Bonar

The Word of God is the basis for any and all ministries in the church. Without it, we have no sword in which to fight, no light in which to see, and no truth in which to proclaim. As ambassadors, we are on a mission to communicate the message of our King; therefore, it is imperative we know what He has declared. Continual and ongoing examination of His Word is the lifework of the minister. As we study the Word of God, we must systematically be on the lookout.

Look Around. See where the Bible book fits in the canon of Scripture. Start wide and move inward. Determine the book's general purpose in God's revelatory plan.

Look In. Take a tour through the entire book and see how each chapter connects with the chosen passage of Scripture. It is at this point, we should consider the thoughts and ideas of the text, and how the meaning is substantiated.

Look Out. Consider the historical and cultural background of the passage. This will help frame the surrounding elements of the text, properly aligning the time and place in which it was written.

Look Up and Down. Know where the text has been and consider where it is going; it is at this point you will have a better idea on where it is.

Look Side to Side. See how each word connects. See how each sentence flows. See how the meaning unfolds through semantics, syntax, and grammar. It is the minister's responsibility to determine how everything in the passage relates to each other.

Look All Over. Cross reference your passage. This will not only provide a systematic and theological framework for your text, it will also demonstrate the richness of God's Word as you show your people the vastness and depth of Scripture.

Look Within. Once the minister of God understands the contextual meaning, he must align his heart, mind, and spirit with his glorious discoveries. Before his message can ever go out to his congregation, it must first go into his own heart. This is the true work of examination: As you examine the Word, the Word begins to examine you.

TAKEAWAYS:

- No matter what the ministry, the Bible is the bedrock for all the servant of God says and does.
- The contextual meaning of the passage is the true meaning; therefore, we must adamantly discover it.
- The Bible does a heart-work in the life of its student.

QUESTIONS:

How do you determine the contextual meaning of a passage?

_____

_____

_____

_____

_____

As you study the Word, what systematic approach do you use?

_____

_____

_____

_____

_____

How does the Bible examine you as you read and study?

_____

_____

_____

_____

_____

PRAYER:

Heavenly Counselor, By Your Word I have been enriched, equipped, and encouraged. There have also been times when Your word has rebuked me, convicted me, and revealed in me certain sins of the heart. As I get into the Word, let the Word get into me. As I examine it more, let it examine me and change me so that I can be a greater minister for You.

MEDITATION

Selected Reading:
Psalm 77, Proverbs 4:23-27, 1 Timothy 4:13-16

"The end of study is to hoard up truth, but of meditation to lay it forth in conference or holy conversation." –Thomas Manton

It was an inconceivable task. Joshua had to mobilize, organize, and unify millions of people across the Jordan river into the land of Canaan. Leading Israel across the waters meant facing cities where the walls were built to the heavens. It meant fighting armies that were fortified and prepared for war. It meant struggling through the complexities of guiding an entire nation into a land where everyone was staking their own territories. How would he be equipped for such an historic task?

One word: Meditation.

The Lord said, "This book of the law shall not depart out of thy mouth; but thou shalt *meditate* therein day and night, that thou mayest observe to do according to all that is written therein: for then thou shalt make thy way prosperous, and then thou shalt have good success" (Joshua 1:8). The triumph of Joshua and the success of Israel hinged upon his willingness to meditate on God's Word.

The same holds true for you and me. It is a weak ministry that gives little thought to the meditation of God's Word; for by it, we are enlightened more fully to the promises and will of God.

Meditation brings Familiarity. Reading God's Word and meditating on God's Word are two different things. The primary difference is that in meditation we retain more of what we read. When we *only read* a passage, we tend to store it away or possibly toss it away; but in meditating upon a passage, we become familiar with the text. We consider it, think about it, we mull over it until the text becomes a part of us.

Meditation births Fellowship. Christ Jesus is the eternal Word, and so, when we flood our minds and thoughts with Scripture, we are opening the doorway into His presence. It is important to implement hermeneutical principles of grammar, context, history, and the such; but the goal of Bible study is ultimately to know Christ and pattern our lives after Him. Meditation of the written Word allows us to draw our hearts closer to the Living Word.

Meditation breeds Fruit. As we meditate, we are planting seeds of truth in our conscience, the Holy Spirit is watering, nurturing, and growing those seeds, the Son is communing with us in those efforts, and God the Father gives the increase. The fruit of meditation yields a harvest of milk and honey. Just ask Joshua.

TAKEAWAYS:

- It's difficult to minister the Word without meditating on it.
- God works through meditation to solidify His promises.
- The greatest fruit of meditation is communion with Christ.

QUESTIONS:

In your own words, define meditation in the Scriptural sense.

_____

_____

_____

_____

_____

How does meditation upon God's Word fit into your scope of study?

_____

_____

_____

_____

_____

How do you think meditation benefits ministry?

_____

_____

_____

_____

_____

PRAYER:

My Lord and Savior, I want to yield fruit that is pleasing and honorable to You. Grant me spiritual insight, discernment, and great understanding of Your Word. Help me to not only ponder the truth of Your Word but guide me to implement the promises of God. Help me to see the necessity of slowing down and thinking upon the truths that You have revealed.

25

ORGANIZATION

Selected Reading:
Exodus 18, Habakkuk 2, Mark 6:35-44

"Go to the ant, thou sluggard;
consider her ways, and be wise." –King Solomon

Efficiency in the ministry is the byproduct of deliberate and strategic organization. "Let all things be done decently and in order" was the admonition of the apostle Paul to a somewhat chaotic and carnal Corinthian church. Each member doing their own thing, their own way, in their own timing did not promote a spiritually healthy environment. On the contrary, such an approach to ministry created a culture of chaos, to which God is never the Author (1 Corinthians 14:33). When God decides to do anything, He writes it out in orderly fashion on the wall. His ministers would be wise to follow suit.

Many well-intended men have failed to execute their God-given assignments because of their inability (or unwillingness) to properly coordinate their efforts. Moses faced this dilemma when he led God's people. Israel's great deliverer thought he had to be the judge over every situation among the people until his father-in-law counseled him to get organized. He advised Moses to teach able-bodied men who could rule and judge over their affairs. Had Moses continued leading them in a disorganized fashion, he would have become both inefficient and depleted, "Thou wilt surely wear away, both thou, and this people that is with thee" (Exodus 18:18).

The Lord modeled an organized public ministry for three years. From sending out His disciples, to visiting strategic cities, to feeding the multitude in groups of fifties and hundreds, He exemplified, in divine fashion, the efficiency of organization.

Such a pattern offers great consolation to the administrators of God's kingdom. The tasks before us are many: Preaching sermons, teaching lessons, equipping disciples, leading ministries, visiting the shut-ins, praying with the sick, shepherding the flock, reaching the world...and the list goes on and on. If we endeavor to fulfill our assignments without proper organization, we will find ourselves tossed about in a sea of inefficiency. Paul Hovey said, "A blind man's world is bounded by the limits of his touch; an ignorant man's world by the limits of his knowledge; a great man's world by the limits of his vision." A vision without organization is nothing more than a daydream that eventually fades away somewhere in the periphery of yesterday's idea.

TAKEAWAYS:

- God's work is not fulfilled with a spirit of confusion.
- When we fail to organize, we exhibit a poor testimony in the work of the Lord.
- Christ is our great example of an organized ministry.

QUESTIONS:

How does organization lead to success?

_____

_____

_____

_____

_____

Do you have a strategic plan for implementing your ministry goals?

_____

_____

_____

_____

_____

How do you coincide strategy with faith?

_____

_____

_____

_____

_____

PRAYER:

Almighty God, You are a God of order, design, and purpose. As I labor in the work of the ministry, remind me of Your example and teach me Your ways. Give me wisdom to properly strategize all the components of ministry so that Your name is glorified. You are not the Author of confusion, therefore, help me to operate with discernment and clarity.

26

COMMUNICATION

Selected Reading:
Proverbs 25:11-13, Acts 20:17-38

"The best talks leave the audience wanting more. Stop talking before the audience stops listening." –Howard Hendricks

The minister of God spends countless hours a week reading, studying, digging, and writing down words. Words from Scripture, words from books, words from preaching, words from prayer and meditation, words from conversations...all these words (hundreds of thousands) are cultivated, processed, and considered as he endeavors to minister to the people of God. The challenge is to take those words and condense them into a message that is relevant, convicting, spiritual, and Scriptural. Therefore, he must ensure that he has the right words. This is a serious task, not only because of the time-constraints we face in this generation, but more importantly, because our words have meaning. Our words have immediate, continual, and eternal influence upon those who hear them. Therefore, we must take caution and use discretion when it comes to our communication. We should put our words to the test.

The Clarity Test. We are not called to impress with our words, we are called to present a clear and concise message from God's Word. When we jumble our words with endless thoughts, we typically distort the truth of Scripture and disengage our listeners.

The Conviction Test. You will never influence people with your words if your words have not first influenced you. Words on our lips are only validated by the witness of our lives. Effective communication must be rooted in personal conviction.

The Creativity Test. We should never compromise truth for creativity; but an effective minister will find ways to illuminate truth in the hearts of his audience. Occasionally, you should join the audience and see if you have anything worth listening to.

The Confidence Test. The confidence of the minister should not be rooted in pride, but rather in knowing our message is validated by the very words of God. If you are not speaking confidently, they will have a hard time listening confidently.

The Consistency Test. Albert Mohler said, "When the real leader shows up, everyone already knows what he is going to say." Repetition of truth provides the framework of trust. When your people hear and see consistency in your message, they will be more apt to follow your leadership.

TAKEAWAYS:

- Our words are weighed in the balance of eternity.
- The minister must evaluate his communication skills.
- Our words must be used to proclaim His Word.

QUESTIONS:

How often do you speak publicly? How do you prepare?

_____

_____

_____

_____

_____

How important is it to know your audience before speaking to them?

_____

_____

_____

_____

_____

What percentage of your ministry is allotted to communication?

_____

_____

_____

_____

_____

PRAYER:

Dear Lord, Give me utterance to speak on your behalf. Season my words with grace and truth. Help me to articulate the grand truths of Scripture every time I minister to Your people. Let the words of my mouth be pleasing to You, O God! And may all I say to others bring glory to Your holy name. Empower me to speak and enlighten men to hear.

27

APPLICATION

Selected Reading:
Acts 8:26-40, 1 Thessalonians 4:1-12

"If preachers never specify where in real life the principles apply, the instruction remains irrelevant abstractions." –Bryan Chapell

There is no shortage of biblical information these days. From books to podcasts, from small groups to collective worship, from conferences to blogs, we have access to information more than any other time in history. The goal of the Christian life, however, is not just to collect a storehouse of information. Somewhere along the way, information must be illuminated in such a way that it causes the believer to act. Herein lies the responsibility of the minister of God.

In his book, *Between Two Worlds*, John Stott warned expositors of God's Word to be cautious in the communicative process. We can be so interested in accurately expositing the text, Stott contends, that we neglect to "earth out the passage to the average parishioner." What he meant was that ministers of God must preset the truth of God's Word so that the hearer can appropriate it in his or her life. Spurgeon said that in many ways, "Application is where the real sermon begins." Ministers must be careful not to tell people what to do without enabling them to do it. Imagine a young toddler transitioning from crawling to walking. If the parents screamed, "Walk! Walk!" to their fledgling child, they would be accurate in their instruction; however, they would not be very helpful. You can tell people *what* to do, *where* to do it, and even *why* to do it, but if you fail to show them *how* to do it, they will be unequipped to walk in truth.

Alexander Maclaren always sat an empty chair across his desk during his exegetical and expositional preparation. In the chair, he would envision an imaginary person and consider how the truth of Scripture would apply to that individual. I submit that we are not preaching to imaginary people; therefore, we must apply truth to real individuals offering real solutions to their real issues.

The greatest way to make application is not only to present a clear, concise way in which to employ truth, but rather to embody the very truth you are presenting. It is difficult to mobilize a church to discipleship if the pastor is not making disciples himself. It is challenging to call a class to prayer if the teacher spends little time in supplication. "Earthing out the passage" will be much easier if the passage has been previously earthed out in the life of the minister before he calls others to apply it.

TAKEAWAYS:

- Information has little value without application.
- Real transformation takes place when truth is applied.
- The most effective application is from a changed life.

QUESTIONS:

What's the difference between information and application?

_____

_____

_____

_____

_____

Do you intentionally apply the truth you preach in your own life?

_____

_____

_____

_____

_____

List any New Testament sermons where application is made:

_____

_____

_____

_____

_____

PRAYER:

Gracious God, You have not only given us truth, You have provided the means in which we can and should apply the truth. What a great privilege it is to be able to show others the life and light of Jesus Christ. Call into my soul the need for others to know and respond to the Word of God. Illuminate in my own heart the message I declare to others.

28

INVITATION

Selected Reading:
Matthew 7:24-29, Revelation 22:14-21

*"Today is when everything that is going to happen
from now on begins." –*Harvey Firestone Jr.

One of the primary objectives of any ministry is to invite people to respond to the truth of God's Word. We can do all the grunt-work of exposition, formulate outlines, properly explain the text, develop interesting illustrations, and even close with practical application, but if we fail to invite people to make decisions, then we cannot be disheartened when they fail to appropriate truth in their lives. People need to be invited.

Jesus clearly understood this important component of ministry. Whenever He preached a message or gave a life-lesson, He always concluded with an invitation. He would appeal to the conscience, the spirit, the intellect, and the heart of His listeners in such a way that they would be forced to make decisions about their condition. The clarion call of His public ministry can be summarized with these welcoming words, "Come unto me, all ye that labor and are heavy laden, and I will give you rest" (Matthew11:28).

Invitations must be Specific. Imagine receiving an invitation in the mail without knowing the date, location, time, or place. If the specifics are not laid out in a precise fashion, you cannot be perturbed when no one shows up to the event. The same is true in ministry. People need to know what they are being invited to.

Invitations must be Scriptural. Every invitation must be rooted in biblical soil. If you invite someone to agree with your opinion, then their decisions will be as volatile as your mood. Ministers must be careful to invite people to the scriptural reality of the text. Any other invitation will inevitably lead to error.

Invitations must be Soulful. We are not appealing to the fleshly emotions of mankind, but to the spirit. The Word of God is spiritually written and must be spiritually discerned. According to Jesus, God is seeking true worshippers to worship in "spirit and in truth" (John 4:23). If we invite people to make decisions in the flesh, we should not be surprised if they produce fleshly fruit.

Invitations must be Soon. The hour cometh when no man can work. Today is the day of salvation. Now is the appointed time. The closing words of Scripture remind the minister of God to hasten the invitation to mankind, "And the Spirit and the bride say, Come. And let him that heareth say, Come." (Revelation 22:17).

TAKEAWAYS:

- Even as Jesus invited people to respond, we are called to bring people to a place of decision.
- Invitations must be clearly and precisely articulated.
- Whatever we are going to do for Christ, we must do now.

QUESTIONS:

Study the preaching of Jesus. How does He conclude His sermons?

_____

_____

_____

_____

_____

How does the Holy Spirit work in the invitation process?

_____

_____

_____

_____

_____

Do you think the statement "People need to be invited" is true?

_____

_____

_____

_____

_____

PRAYER:

Lord and Savior, I realize that only the Spirit of God can quicken and make Your Word alive in people's hearts, but as a minister of the gospel, show me how I can more effectively invite people to the realities of Your truth. I pray the power of God would manifest itself in me through prayer and meditation.

29

MOBILIZATION

Selected Reading:
Joshua 6, Nehemiah 3, Romans 16

*"No one can whistle a symphony; it takes
an orchestra to play it."* –Alford E. Luccock

When was the last time you heard a sermon about
Aristarchus? Can you recall any songs that may
include Epaphras or Onesimus? Do you have any
books that chronicle the lives of Tychicus or Erastus? Are you
familiar with Urbane, Quartus, Sosipater, or Phlegon? No, these
are not names on the Periodic Table of Elements. These are just a
few individuals whom the apostle Paul mobilized to fulfill his
work in the ministry.

Outside of Jesus Christ, no other man in history had more
influence and impact with the gospel. From building churches, to
discipling converts, to itinerate preaching, to missionary journeys,
to writing epistles, to equipping the saints...the fingerprints of
Paul are all over the work of the New Testament. However, Paul
had the unique ability to engage the handiwork of others in the
work of God's kingdom. His prints were not alone.

129

In every city, in every church, in every ministry, he uniquely mobilized his band of brothers (and sisters) with strategic gospel planning. He intentionally brought others along for the journey, equipping and discipling them to equip and disciple others.

Mobilization is the keen ability to position people in key roles of leadership and service. Mobilization is not just about getting someone to help you out; it is about having the right people in the right place for the right purpose. Consider the following:

- Mobilization is *not* about having people in place.
- Mobilization is *not* about having the *right people* in place.
- Mobilization is *not* about having people in the *right place.*

I repeat, mobilization requires having the *right* people in the *right* working for the *right* purpose. D.L. Moody said, "I would rather get ten men to do the right job than to do the job of ten men." When this spiritual dynamic of mobilization takes place in the church, there will be no limit to the amount of fruit that can be harvested by the collected efforts.

We should thank God for the ministry of men like Paul, Peter, James, and John. But the truth is, we need to mobilize some men like Patrobas, Hermes, and Andronicus (Romans 16), and some women like Euodias and Syntyche (Philippians 4) for the work of the Lord. Without them, the burden of ministry is harder to bear.

TAKEAWAYS:

- We can't just preach to people; we must position them.
- Every member must be situated by their giftedness.
- When everyone has the same goal, the process is easier.

QUESTIONS:

Who are the individuals around you that help coordinate ministry?

_____

_____

_____

_____

_____

How do you determine the right person for the right position?

_____

_____

_____

_____

_____

How do you motivate others to help bear the load of ministry?

_____

_____

_____

_____

_____

PRAYER:

Almighty God, I want to thank You for the co-laborers I have in ministry. I pray that You will give us a spirit of unity as we strive together for the furtherance of the gospel. Help me to equip them, train them, lead them, and mobilize them so that Your name will be glorified in all we do. Amen.

CONTINUATION

Selected Reading:
Psalm 13, Isaiah 40:28-31, Galatians 6:7-10

"Perseverance is the hard work you do after you get tired of doing the hard work you've already done." –Newt Gingrich

William Carey, the father of modern missions, left England in 1793 to preach the gospel in India. He spent years learning indigenous languages and translating the Bible in Sanskrit. On March 11, 1812 he lost most of his literary work to a fire in his print shop. Carey had a wide collection of items he had personally written. The fire consumed ten different translations of the Bible, two grammar books, a large supply of dictionaries, deeds, and accounting books, and most unfortunately, his completed Sanskrit dictionary.

After the fire, Carey was faced with the daunting task of reproducing his material. Instead of *whining*, he started *writing*. Line by line, page by page, book by book. Carey himself said of his work, "It is easier to walk a road the second time." At the end of his ministry, William Carey had translated the Bible, either in whole or part, into forty-four different languages.

Carey labored in India for seven years before he saw one soul converted to Christ. While many of his supporters and financial backers were ready to give up on his gospel adventure, Carey continued with deep conviction. He famously said of himself, "If he gives me credit for being a plodder, he will describe me justly. Anything beyond that will be too much. I can plod. I can persevere in any definite pursuit."

I. Can. Plod.

Those three mono-syllable words are profoundly powerful. Every minister of God, like Carey, will be tempted to quit at some point in the journey. The fiery trials will come. The barren seasons will be extended. The very core of our faith will be challenged.

- What do you do when there are no converts?
- What do you do when preaching falls on deaf ears?
- What do you do when finances are running low?
- What do you do when others tell you to quit?

I exhort you to plod on! Continue! Keep going! Press ahead! Move forward no matter the cost. We are not doing what we do for earthly results or recognition, but rather we gladly plod so that one day we will hear the crowned King of Glory say, "Well done, thou good and faithful servant" (Matthew 25:21).

TAKEAWAYS:

- Success in the ministry is determined by faithfulness.
- Obey God and leave the results to Him.
- The reward of ministry is not measured in earthly terms.

QUESTIONS:

Do you ever feel exhausted or depleted in the work of God?

_____

_____

_____

_____

_____

How do trials affect your work ethic?

_____

_____

_____

_____

_____

What area of ministry are you "plodding" in right now? Explain.

_____

_____

_____

_____

_____

PRAYER:

Heavenly Father, I confess that at times I feel like I am plodding more than I am producing. I get impatient at the lack of results. I grow weary at the indifference of Your people. I become frustrated with my own spirituality. During those times, help me to plod along. Help me to continue in the work of the Lord, knowing that my reward awaits.

PART 4:
THE COMMUNION
OF THE MINISTER

31

ON CALL WITH THE LORD

Selected Reading:

Joshua 1, Judges 6:1-24, Psalm 11

"I must take care above all that I cultivate communion with Christ." –Charles Spurgeon

hat are you doing for the Lord? That sounds like a spiritual question, does it not? It is one that might possibly be asked in the halls of ministerial gatherings. Perhaps it is a question you have even asked yourself on occasion. Such an inquiry may be posed with good intentions, but I assure you, it is the wrong question to ask God's servant.

Over the course of my ministry (and through my own mistakes) I have discovered this subtle but profound nuance: The Lord never calls us to do something *for* Him; He only calls us to do something *with* Him.

God's objective for your life and ministry is not for you to merely fulfill assignments. He is not looking for a subcontractor to produce numbers, meet quotas, and fill out paperwork. His calling *for* your life is not detached from His communion *in* your life. Above all else, God has called you to be with Him. It is through communion, fellowship, and intimacy that God equips us for His ordained work. The work He has called us to do cannot be fulfilled apart from His abiding presence.

Before God sent Moses into Egypt, He invited Him to stand on the hallowed ground of His presence at the burning bush. Before he could *go* for the Lord, Moses had to *come* to the Lord. God would do His own work, He simply invited Moses to be with Him during the process. God said the same thing to Joshua, "Have not I commanded thee...for the LORD thy God is with thee whithersoever thou goest" (Joshua 1:9). He has given the same promise to us as well, "Go ye therefore, and teach all nations...and lo, I am with thee always, even unto the end of the world" (Matthew 28:18-21).

When God invites us to an assignment, He first and foremost invites us to Himself. Therefore, the true joy of ministry is not necessarily what we do *for* the Lord, it is the fact that we get to do what we do *with* the Lord.

TAKEAWAYS:

- God calls us to Himself before calling us to anything else.
- Communion with God is the heartbeat of any ministry.
- God doesn't expect us to do something detached from His abiding presence.
- Your communion with God will equip you for any and all assignments He may give you in your life.

QUESTIONS:

By what terms do you measure success in the ministry?

_____

_____

_____

_____

_____

Is your communion with Christ the catalyst for weekly obligations?

_____

_____

_____

_____

Do you ever feel like you are working by yourself? If so, explain.

_____

_____

_____

_____

_____

PRAYER:

My Lord and God, I realize that above all else, You want me to know You, to experience You, to be in fellowship with You. Please do not allow my ministerial obligations to become a substitute for my relationship with You.

32

POSITIONED FOR COMMUNION

Selected Reading:

Psalm 1, John 10:28-38, Romans 12:1-3

"We all want to spend eternity with God; we just don't want to spend time with Him." –Mark Batterson

Our relationship with the Lord can be described in two words: Union and communion. Our *union* with Christ took place at conversion. This is a positional truth. We are in Christ and Christ is in us. This is the hope of glory. This is the lifeblood of us being in His family. We are alive because Christ is alive, and we are in Christ. Such a glorious union can never be altered, changed, or undone.

Our *communion*, however, speaks of the condition of that union relationship. Communion with Christ is the recognition of God's grace in our lives and our willingness to love Him, serve Him, and obey Him. Our *union* with Christ is a divine work alone (we did not and could not save ourselves); *communion* with Christ is also a divine work yet it factors in human responsibility. Communion calls our attention to the union we have in Christ and then challenges us to respond. Communion, by definition alone, is the act in which two parties voluntarily agree to engage one another. Sadly, it is possible to have union in the Lord while having very little communion with the Lord.

This is true of any relationship, but especially in marriage. Legally speaking, you cannot be any less or any more married to your spouse (this is your union); but you can have a stronger or weaker marriage based upon your willingness to invest in that relationship (this is your communion).

For the believer, you can't be any more or any less saved than you already are; but you can have more joy or less joy in your relationship with God based upon the degree of communion you have with Christ. "God cannot give us more than he already has given us in Christ, we are complete in him," said John MacArthur, "the believer's need, therefore, is not to receive something more but to do something more with what he or she has."

When we truly see all that we are in Christ, and when we fully discover all that Christ is in us, we will find joyful communion flowing from our eternal union.

TAKEAWAYS:

- Our positional union in Christ gives way for our ongoing communion with Christ.
- Union and communion are both works of God's grace; union speaks of faith in Christ while communion speaks of fellowship with Christ.
- The level of communion I have with God varies based upon the degree of devotion I have for the Lord.

QUESTIONS:

In your own words, describe the basis for communion with God.

_____

_____

_____

_____

_____

In what ways can your communion with God grow and develop?

_____

_____

_____

_____

_____

Is communion with God solely the responsibility of the believer?

_____

_____

_____

_____

_____

PRAYER:

Lord God, I thank You for salvation. You have redeemed me and washed me clean with the blood of the Lamb. As your child, I am grateful to be part of Your family. May my union with You be the driving force of my ongoing communion with You.

33

THIRSTING FOR GOD

Selected Reading:
Deuteronomy 4, Psalm 27, Matthew 5:1-12

*"The most vital question for all those who claim to be a Christian is this:
Do they have a soul thirst for God?"* –Martyn Lloyd Jones

There is something called the "Rule of Three" when it comes to survival. An individual can last three minutes without air, three hours in extreme heat or cold, three weeks without food, and three days without water. After three days without water, the body begins breaking down physically and psychologically. When dehydration sets in, one can expect to experience the following: A dry mouth, a swollen tongue, fatigue in the legs, dizziness, fainting, palpitations of the heart, confusion, severe headaches, tightness in the chest, and above all, an insatiable thirst.

Thirst: This is the most common way to know if you are depleted of fluids. When someone is dehydrated, they will develop an insatiable desire for water. I suppose the same thing can be said about the soul. In Psalm 42, David experienced a deep thirst in his heart for God. In the middle of the wilderness, he cried out:

"As the hart panteth after the waterbrooks, so panteth my soul after thee, O God. My soul thirsteth for God, for the living God: when shall I come and appear before God" (Psalm 42:1)

David's desire for God is illustrated as a deer on the run. It is searching, longing, yearning for the stream of gladness. Only there will it satisfy its craving, only there will it quench its thirst. Dry, distant, and facing potential death, the hart makes its move toward the brook. It had been there before, and if it were going to survive among the harsh elements, it would have to taste of the brook again.

Just as water is essential for survival in the natural realm, communion with God is infinitely vital for soul survival. We must earnestly and continually hunger and thirst for the deep things of God. E.M. Bounds said, "Without desire, there is no burden of soul, no sense of need, no ardency, no vision, no strength, no glow of faith. There is no mighty pressure, no holding on to God." Perhaps more importantly, there is no quenching of the heart. But for those who hunger and thirst after righteousness there is a glorious promise: They shall be filled!

TAKEAWAYS:

- Believers can become distant from God.
- Our thirst for the Lord should be continual and ongoing.
- All the spiritual sustenance we need comes from an intimate and personal relationship with the Lord.
- Desire is the catalyst for being filled by God.

QUESTIONS:

Is there a time when you felt closer to God than you do now?

_____

_____

_____

_____

_____

Is your thirst for God greater than your thirst for other things?

_____

_____

_____

_____

_____

What does it mean to have your thirst quenched by God?

_____

_____

_____

_____

_____

PRAYER:

O God, Sustainer of my life, I long to know You more deeply, to experience Your presence more fully, and to obey Your Word more faithfully. Lead me in the paths of righteousness and help me to pursue the spiritual water brooks of the soul.

34

TEARING DOWN IDOLS

Selected Reading:
Exodus 20:1-6, Isaiah 44:9-20, Galatians 5:19-21

*"When something good becomes an idol, the pleasure
it brings dies in the process."* –Kyle Idleman

I dolatry is so repugnant in the mind of God that when He constituted Israel's moral, civil, and religious guidelines, He commanded that they worship Him, and Him alone as the premise of the entire law. Jesus affirmed this when He called it the "first and great commandment." This commandment not only secured the spiritual well-being of the individual, but on a much larger scale, it served as the spiritual bedrock of Israel's society. God reiterated this commandment to His people when they came into the land of Canaan. If they loved, worshipped, and served the Lord God alone, they would have blessing upon their lives. But if they turned their hearts to false gods they would be cursed.

Aaron experienced first-hand the problematic nature of idol worship for those in leadership. When Moses came down from receiving the law, he discovered that his brother permitted the children of Israel to fashion a golden calf. By the time Moses reached the congregation, they were dancing and attributing their deliverance to the golden image. With rage and fury, Moses broke the tablets of stones and executed 3000 individuals that day. The ultimatum was given, "Who is on the Lord's side?"

It's hard to imagine that a minister of God would struggle with the sin of idolatry, but such a scenario is a real threat. Do you have idols? We say "no" because we believe having idols involves living among the heathen in the back jungles of third-world countries or bowing before oddly shaped blocks of wood and stone. But the truth is, neatly tucked away in the untamed desires of our lives, abide those things that compete with God's throne.

An idol is anything that we love, desire, turn to, and invest in more than we do our relationship with God. Ironically, however, an idol, by Hebrew definition, literally means "good for nothing; worthless; having no value." How is it possible that we could give so much of our love and affection to something that has no value over a God Who is infinitely and immeasurably good, and bestows good gifts to us? Tear down those shrines in your heart. Rip the curtain that secretly conceals those false gods. Turn over the tables of idol worship and denounce anything that attempts to usurp God's authority. He is jealous for you; be jealous of Him.

TAKEAWAYS:

- Anything that supersedes my love for God is idolatry.
- Idolatry leads to vain, empty, joyless living.
- I must intentionally oppose anything that competes with my love and affection for God.

QUESTIONS:

What does it mean to "have no other gods" before the Lord?

_____

_____

_____

_____

_____

Have you ever dealt with idolatry in your life? Ministry?

_____

_____

_____

_____

_____

What are the necessarily steps of eliminating idols of the heart?

_____

_____

_____

_____

_____

PRAYER:

Dear Lord, You are God alone. Only You deserve my attention, my affection, and my adoration. Examine my heart to see if there be any wicked thing in me. Expose the idols of my life and by Your grace help me to tear down anything that may try to take Your place.

35

BE STILL AND KNOW

Selected Reading:
1 Samuel 12, Psalm 46, Luke 6:12-16

*"Our meditation must be directed toward God; otherwise we may
spend our time in quiet conversation with ourselves."* –A.W. Tozer

Devotional writer Oswald Chambers said, "If God allows you to be stripped of the exterior portions of your life, He means for you to cultivate the interior." Cultivating the interior is the essence of communion with God. It is, as David MacIntyre puts it, the time in which we "discover the excellence of God's character, and by beholding Him we also allow Him to transform the soul." If the soul needs "interior cultivation" then devotion is the soil in which it takes root.

This all sounds lovely, desirable even; but so many Christians, even spiritual leaders miss out on the most vital aspect of their faith: devotion to God. What is required in devotion? Why do so many miss out on this interior cultivation?

Devotion requires a quiet place. We are addicted to noise. We wake up to a screeching alarm only to go to bed with a roaring television. We need a place of retreat. We need a place where all the superficialities of this life fade into periphery of God's glory. Do you have a place to go to spend time alone with God? If not, find one today, stake your ground, claim your borders, kick off your sandals, and draw nigh to the holy place.

Devotion requires a quiet hour. Jerry Bridges said, "Just as a house must have a foundation and framework to hold it together, so our all-day communion with God must have a foundation and a framework to hold it together. The foundation of our communion with God is the morning quiet time." The morning is designed by God to find mercy anew. It is suggested by Christ Himself that we find the Heavenly Father early. Praying for "daily bread" does the body little good in the evening after the day is spent. Christ's command to pray places a priority on a particular period: the morning time. Rise early, and often; find God before the frustrations of the day find you.

Devotion requires a quiet heart. Steve Farrar contends, "It is entirely possible for a man to appear perfectly fine, to live an outward life of doing all the right things, and yet to be completely isolated from God in his heart." Devotion is about getting your heart in tune with God; again, and again, and again. To do such a thing, we must hear the soft melody of the Master as He plays to our soul in quiet solitude.

TAKEAWAYS:

- Communion with God gives opportunity for faith to grow.
- A quiet place, a quiet hour, and a quiet heart are essential.
- Distractions of this life divert our attention from God.

QUESTIONS:

Do you have a specific devotional time with God? When and Where?

_____

_____

_____

_____

_____

What is the true objective of spending alone time with the Lord?

_____

_____

_____

_____

_____

Can you identify any hinderances that prevent you from devotion?

_____

_____

_____

_____

_____

PRAYER:

Dear Father, I pray for consistency and commitment when it comes to my devotional time with You. May I be intentional in scheduling my life and ministry as to leave plenty of time for communion. May that time be spent in sweet fellowship, and may You cultivate the interior of my heart.

36

AT HOME IN THE HEART

Selected Reading:

Psalm 51, Proverbs 3, Jeremiah 17:9-10

*"The Lord has two heavens to dwell in, and the
holy heart is one of them."* –Thomas Watson

For everyone who has faith in Jesus Christ, they are secured, sealed unto the day of redemption. We are crucified with Christ, nevertheless we live because Christ lives in us. (Galatians 2:20). We are His tabernacle, we are His temple, we are His body. The question, then, is not whether Christ is in us, He is. The real question is this: Is Christ at home in us?

Augustine said, "Narrow is the mansion of my soul; enlarge Thou it, that Thou mayest enter in." In so many words, he was asking the Lord to give him a big heart so that he could better accommodate the abode of God. Such is the request of the sincere follower of Christ: Dear Lord, make room in my heart for you! More room, more space, more time, more thought, more contemplation! Clear out the unnecessary and trivial clutter so that my whole being is overwhelmed with thy presence. Make my heart bigger so that you are more at home.

This was also the prayer of the apostle Paul for the Ephesian believers. Wanting them to be filled with the "bigness" and fullness of God, he requested:

> "That Christ may dwell in your hearts by faith; that ye, being rooted and grounded in love, May be able to comprehend with all saints what *is* the breadth, and length, and depth, and height; And to know the love of Christ, which passeth knowledge, that ye might be filled with all the fulness of God" (Ephesians 3:17-19)

I wonder if Christ is at home in us. How unhospitable it would be for the Lord to feel like an unwelcomed guest in His own house. Are there things that lurk in the recesses of our hearts that would make Christ uncomfortable? Do we crowd His living room with our worldly possessions and natural desires? How big is your heart? You may say not very big, and you might be right. But you can, as Augustine did, ask God to enlarge it. Tozer said, "The widest thing in the universe is not space; it is the potential capacity of the human heart. Being made in the image of God, it is capable of almost unlimited extension in all directions." Ask God to stretch it so that His presence may fill it; and that He would be at home in you.

TAKEAWAYS:

- It's possible for Christ to be in us but not be at home in us.
- The heart can become crowded with the things of this life.
- We can and should pray for the love of Christ and the fullness of God to dwell in our hearts.

QUESTIONS:

Do you think that Christ is "at home" in your heart this moment?

_____

_____

_____

_____

_____

What does the "fullness of God" mean to you?

_____

_____

_____

_____

_____

What else lives in our heart with Christ? Explain your answer.

_____

_____

_____

_____

_____

PRAYER:

Dear Lord, I ask You to reveal anything in my heart that may grieve You in anyway. Help me not to crowd my soul with worldly desires and ambitions. Be at home in me, find Your resting place, and enlarge me heart to know You more.

37

MEETING GOD IN THE WORD

Selected Reading:

Psalm 19:7-11, Hebrews 14:12-14, 2 Timothy 3:15-17

"When reading a book in a dark room, you take it to the window for more light. So take your Bibles to Christ." –Robert M'Cheyne

I magine just for a moment the Word of God as a continent, undiscovered in your heart and mind. Walk the lush fields of gold and see the abundant harvest of truth. Hike the mountainous peaks that rise above those fields until you come to the apex of wonder. Look out in amazement as far as your eye will permit. See the lowlands beneath and scout the course from above. Who can know every winding path that scurries from each offsetting trail?

As you sink down to the canyons, take time to rest along the streaming rivers and feel the rush of waves over your soul. Sit under the shade of the trees of life. Take of their fruit and satisfy your hunger until you have the strength to press on.

Descend, further still, into the crevice's and discover the rich treasures below. Plow your way through the impervious soil until you have the holy resources in your hands. Come up for air until the very breath of God fills your lungs. With newfound treasure, take the precious stones with you as you continue your journey. Trek your way through every grassy hill, every golden plain, every holy holler. At every turn, walk in the newness of truth's terrain. What immeasurable treasure we have in the Holy Word of God!

In God's Word we not only have access to the truth, but we are promised communion with the Truth-Giver. Like the disciples who walked the Emmaus Road, our hearts will burn within us when we fellowship with Christ over His Word. To have Him expound His mysteries in the deep places of our heart is the most rapturous experience this side of glory. Is this not the promise of Christ Himself, "These things have I spoken unto you, that my joy might remain in you, and that your joy might be full" (John 15:11).

Full joy, burning hearts, sweet fellowship…these are things the world is dying to experience. Yet, they are only discovered in the pages of holy writ as we commune with Him from day to day. As ministers of His Word, let us be cognizant of this one thing: The view of God's Word is much more enjoyable when you are sharing it with the Tour Guide!

TAKEAWAYS:

- The Bible is an immeasurable treasure that can never be exhausted.
- My communion with Christ cannot be developed apart from ongoing time in His Word.
- There is spiritual joy and fellowship in the living Word.

QUESTIONS:

Do you read your Bible intentionally for communion with Christ?

_____

_____

_____

_____

_____

How much of your ministry time is allocated to scriptural study?

_____

_____

_____

_____

_____

What does it mean to refer to Jesus as the Word of God? Explain.

_____

_____

_____

_____

_____

PRAYER:

Dear Lord, Your Word is a lamp unto my feet, a light unto my path. May I not only discover the treasures found within the pages of Scripture but let me have fellowship with You during the process. Thank You for the precious, life-sustaining, holy Word of God!

38

THE PURPOSE OF PRAYER

Selected Reading:

Matthew 6:5-15, Luke 22:39-46, Hebrews 14:12-14

"Every Christian needs a half hour of prayer each day
except when he is busy, then he needs an hour." –Francis de Sales

W hen we read Scripture we have the opportunity to hear from God; when we pray we have the opportunity to speak to God. Scripture and prayer go hand in hand in the life of the minister. It is the Word of God that equips us to pray; it is prayer that enables us to know more fully the Word. It is at the intersection of Scripture and prayer that we find our sweetest communion. It is there that God waits for us, to hear from us, to speak to us, to empower us. Tozer said:

"It is not reading the Scripture in the original languages or in some contemporary version that makes us better Christians. Rather, it is getting on our knees with the Scriptures spread before us and allowing the Holy Spirit of God to break our hearts. Then, when we have been thoroughly broken before God Almighty, we get up off our knees, go out into the world and proclaim the glorious message of Jesus Christ, the Savior of the world."

Simply put: Prayer is the conduit for spiritual vitality in the life work of God's children. "To be a Christian without prayer," said Martin Luther, "is no more possible than to be alive without breathing." When we breath in Scripture and breath out our prayers, we will experience true life in Jesus Christ.

I have often found myself despondent, perplexed, tired, and exhausted only to go into the prayer closet and become invigorated with the presence of God. It is behind the veil of that holy place I can take the veil off my face as Moses did in the tabernacle and just be my "authentic self." Who *better* to spend time with than the One Who knows me *better* than anyone else?

The truth is, I can preach, I can labor, I can coordinate, I can strategize, I can study, I can do I all I'm obligated to do, but if I do not pray I have truly missed the whole point. Prayer is "where the action is," said John Wesley, "God does nothing except in answer to prayer." The work of prayer continues until death, never perfected in this life. Only in death will our prayers reach the state of perfect maturity. It is in that heavenly hour that our prayers achieve the ultimate goal: To be in the perpetual and uninterrupted presence of God. Until then, we prepare our heart for that moment by continual and ongoing communion with the Lord.

TAKEAWAYS:

- Scripture and prayer are inexplicably connected.
- Strength and power for ministry is fueled by prayer.
- Prayer is not just about getting my needs met, it is about having communion and fellowship with God.

QUESTIONS:

How would you describe the condition of your prayer life?

_____

_____

_____

_____

_____

Explain the relationship between Scripture reading and prayer:

_____

_____

_____

_____

_____

In your own words, how does prayer equip you for the work of God?

_____

_____

_____

_____

_____

PRAYER:

Heavenly Father, what consolation it brings to my heart to know that You hear and answer my prayer. Help me to realize that prayer is more than just getting my needs met, more importantly, it is the opportunity to spend time with You in communion. Guide my heart and mind toward more intimacy and fellowship in prayer.

39

FRUITFUL FELLOWSHIP

Selected Reading:
Isaiah 57, Psalm 4, 2 Corinthians 6

*"Our love to God is measured by our everyday fellowship
with Him and the love it displays."* –Andrew Murray

R each the world with the gospel. Teach the nations. Go into Jerusalem, Judea, Samaria, and unto the uttermost. Baptize new believers. Make disciples. Expect trials.

Can you imagine how overwhelming these commands must have been in those initial moments of receiving the Great Commission. Just a handful of "ignorant and unlearned" men who had no formal training in networking, administration, or theology; and yet, they were called to turn the world upside down with the gospel.

I suppose there must have been some discussion after Jesus ascended. Perhaps the question of "how" came up as a topic of conversation. *How* in the world would they reach the nations? *How* would they be able to establish new converts, baptize them, train them, equip them, all while organizing outreach efforts beyond Jerusalem? *How* would they be able to produce such fruits of righteousness? I would submit that somewhere in the disciple's dilemma they remembered the words of Christ from just a few days prior:

> "Abide in me, and I in you. As the branch cannot bear fruit of itself, except it abide in the vine; no more can ye, except ye abide in me. I am the vine, ye *are* the branches: He that abideth in me, and I in him, the same bringeth forth much fruit: for without me ye can do nothing" (John 15:4-5).

The disciple's fruit would be produced through their fellowship with the Lord. In the Upper Room discourse, the word "abide" was used by Christ eight times in just a few statements. Even as a branch receives its fruit-producing sustenance through the vine, the disciples would be fruitful only through their willingness to abide in Christ. The disciples were not known for their articulation, theological degrees, or handle on the Greek and Hebrew languages; but when they were brought before the counsel, it was obvious to those Jewish leaders that the disciples "had been with Jesus" (Acts 4:13).

Their fruit was produced through their fellowship. The same holds true for His disciples today.

TAKEAWAYS:

- Without Christ we have no spiritual sustenance or power to produce fruit.
- Fruit is the overflow of the man who abides in Christ.
- Your communion with Jesus will be obvious to others.

QUESTIONS:

In your own words, discuss what it means to abide in Christ?

_____

_____

_____

_____

_____

How does your fellowship with Christ fit into your outreach efforts?

_____

_____

_____

_____

_____

What do you think characterizes your ministry above all else?

_____

_____

_____

_____

_____

PRAYER:

Holy Father, I want to see much fruit, and fruit that remains in my life and ministry. Help me to remember that without You I can do nothing. I want to have fruitful fellowship with You. May others see in my life that I have spent time with You.

40

TO BE LIKE CHRIST

Selected Reading:

Genesis 1:26-31, 1 Corinthians 15:51-58

"The good that God works in our lives is conformity
to the likeness of His Son." –Jerry Bridges

Holiness is a divine attribute that can only be imparted to us and through us by our standing and position in Christ. An unsaved person cannot be holy. A saved person can only be holy in Christ (salvation), and through his willingness to submit to the Holy Spirit (sanctification). Holiness is not measured by how stark or different we are from the world because the world is always changing; rather we measure our holiness by our resemblance to Jesus.

Be certain, there is a self-promoting, legalistic brand of holiness that leads to arrogance, conceit, and even false salvation. Andrew Murray warned of this when he said, "There is no pride so dangerous, none so subtle and insidious as the pride of holiness." True holiness, the kind exhibited by Christ, flows from a spirit of righteousness, not self-righteousness (1 Peter 1:16). Therefore, holiness in the life of the believer is the pursuit of adapting to the character of God. This is accomplished through our communion with Christ. Think about it, what is the end goal of the Christian life? Is it to escape hell? Is it to spend eternity in God's heavenly kingdom? Is it to be free from the bondage of sin? Is it to experience joy and peace here on earth? I would contend that all those realities are part of our redemption. However, consider the following verses from God's Word:

- Romans 8:29: "For whom he did foreknow, he also did predestinate to be conformed to the image of his Son,"
- Colossians 1:28: "...that we may present every man perfect in Christ Jesus:"
- 1 John 3:2: "but we know that, when he shall appear, we shall be like him; for we shall see him as he is."

God has *saved* us to *make* us just like Jesus. This is true in our conversion, this is true in our consecration, and this is true in our final consummation. Communion with the Lord, therefore, is the means of grace to help us live like Jesus lived, love like Jesus loved, lead like Jesus led, so that one day we will ultimately look like Jesus looks.

TAKEAWAYS:

- Holiness is an instant work at salvation and an ongoing work through sanctification.
- Holiness is the act of developing the character of God.
- Likeness to Jesus Christ is cultivated through communion. This is the ultimate goal of the Christian life.

QUESTIONS:

In your own words, define the meaning of holiness:

_____

_____

_____

_____

_____

How does God conform us into the image of His Son?

_____

_____

_____

_____

_____

How does communion with Christ develop our likeness to Christ?

_____

_____

_____

_____

_____

PRAYER:

Almighty God, I long to be more like Jesus. I desire to be holy even as You are holy. There are areas of my life that need Your grace. Conform me now into the image of Christ and help me to live in accordance with Your Holy Word.

PART 5:
THE COMPANIONS OF THE MINISTER

THE FAMILY CIRCLE

Selected Reading:
Deuteronomy 6:4-25, 1 Corinthians 16:15-19

*"The happiest moments of my life have been the ones I have
spent at home in the bosom of my family."* –Thomas Jefferson

Every minister of God has a community of people that
surround him, assist him, and need him according to the
divine purposes placed upon his life. Contrary to
monastic theology, the Lord does not call and equip an individual
for isolation. The very nature of God is relational in that He is a
Triune Person eternally existing in the holy community of Father,
Son, and Spirit. Created in the very image of God, we are designed
for interaction. We live, breath, serve, and minister in the specific
communities in which we have been called.

Regardless of a man's platform, popularity, or influential reach,
his first and primary responsibility is to the individuals in his own
home. As a matter of fact, his ability to shepherd his family is
what qualifies him to shepherd the flock of God. Paul said, "For if
a man know not how to rule his own house, how shall he take care
of the church of God?" (1 Timothy 3:5). Many gifted, sought-

after, charismatic leaders have forfeited their right to ministry because they have misaligned their responsibilities in the home. If a man builds a large, thriving ministry at the expense of losing his family, he has not only failed *in* the ministry, he has failed *the* ministry…his first ministry.

To safeguard our families against such tragedy, the Word of God gives us holy counsel. In Titus 1:6-16, the apostle Paul gave qualifications for the minister of God. Above all else, we must be blameless. From this one point, Paul detailed how that plays out in every facet of our lives:

- Be holy, be sober, be just, be temperate, etc.
- Be hospitable, be faithful, be apt to teach, etc.
- Be *not* self-willed, be *not* a brawler, be *not* covetous, etc.

One thing is interesting from that list of credentials: Paul doesn't necessarily tell us what we ought to do, but rather instructs us on what we ought to be. In the ministry, *what we are* is greater than *what we do*. In essence, our character controls our conduct. No one will know this better about our lives than those who sit across our dinner table each evening in the family circle.

TAKEAWAYS:

- A man can only minister to those outside of his family in relation to the way he ministers to those in his family.
- Tragedy strikes the home when it is not intentionally safeguarded and protected.
- What we are is more important than what we do.

QUESTIONS:

Do you feel that responsibilities for family and ministry conflict?

_____

_____

_____

_____

_____

Are you intentionally developing the faith of your family?

_____

_____

_____

_____

_____

How has your family blessed your ministry, and vice-versa?

_____

_____

_____

_____

_____

PRAYER:

Heavenly Father, I am so thankful for the family you have given me. Help me to lead them in accordance with Your Word. Show me how to intentionally invest and involve myself in their lives. Grow our faith together and use us for Your honor and glory.

42

THE HEAVENLY HELPMATE

Selected Reading:

1 Corinthians 13, Colossians 3:12-25, 1 John 4

*"As God by creation made two of one, so by marriage
He made one of two."* –Thomas Adams

When the Lord wanted to reveal the deep mystery of His bond with the church, He likened it unto a marriage. We are the Bride of Christ and He is the Groom. When God instituted the first union between Adam and Eve, He established a heavenly pattern that would ultimately be fulfilled in the church's union with Jesus Christ in redemption. The apostle Paul said it like this:

> "For we are members of his body, of his flesh, and of his bones. For this cause shall a man leave his father and mother, and shall be joined unto his wife, and they two shall be one flesh. This is a great mystery: but I speak concerning Christ and the church" (Ephesians 5:30-32).

These words were originally spoken by God to Adam and Eve in the garden. God gave Adam a companion in Eve, equipped them with His Word, and commanded them to be fruitful and multiply.

Immediately after this, Satan entered the garden of their lives and brought division and destruction to the first parents.

The truth is, not much has changed since the initial fall. Satan absolutely hates marriage. He hates *your* marriage. He despises the love, the unity, and the bond of husband and wife. His hatred of marriage is rooted in his hatred of Christ's love for His church.

I have no statistical data to present here, but I suspect that if the enemy tries to hinder and destroy any and all marriages, he especially targets those who labor and minister in the Word. The minister of the Lord must pay special attention to this matter and see His companion as an instrument of grace bestowed upon his life. He must combat the devices of Satan by following Christ's example of sacrificial love. Martin Luther said, "Let the wife make the husband glad to come home and let him make her sorry to see him leave." Before a man can be that kind of husband to his wife, he must learn to be that kind of bride to His Savior.

A man who genuinely loves the Lord, will more readily and naturally be able to fulfill his ministerial obligations to his wife. When we love, cherish, and nourish our companions we are not only meeting their spiritual and emotional needs, we are revealing the ultimate expression of Christ's love to His own Body.

TAKEAWAYS:

- God established marriage; therefore, Satan attacks it.
- Love for my bride reflects Christ's love for the church.
- My relationship with my bride grows as my relationship with Christ gets stronger.

QUESTIONS:

How does the marriage union testify of Christ's love for His Church?

_____

_____

_____

_____

_____

In what ways do you express the love of Christ to your bride?

_____

_____

_____

_____

_____

What kind of spiritual assaults has your marriage experienced?

_____

_____

_____

_____

_____

PRAYER:

Dear Lord, I want to express my gratitude for the companion You have sent into my life. Help me to be the kind of husband that reflects the very love of Christ. Strengthen my relationship with You so that my relationship with my bride will grow stronger. Guard our home and our marriage with Your love and grace.

43

CHILDREN OF GOD

Selected Reading:
Joshua 4:20-24, 2 Samuel 6:1-12, Proverbs 22

"The parent's life is the child's copybook." –John Partridge

Michelangelo worked on forty-four statues throughout his life; but only finished fourteen, the most popular being his depiction of David. There is a museum in Italy that houses the other unfinished works of the great artist. These "statues" are basically just blocks of stone. They are rarely acknowledged and seldom applauded. It wasn't that Michelangelo lacked talent or skill to complete these projects; he just didn't invest the time needed to bring them to life. I suppose the difference between a masterpiece and a "piece of mass" is the amount of attention, energy, and patience one is willing to invest.

The same holds true with parenting our children. The Lord gives us the responsibility to develop, mold, and shape their identity. We are not only fashioning them to be members of our family, but more importantly, to be members of the family of God. Cotton Mather said, "Children are immortal souls whom God hath,

189

for a time, entrusted to your care, that you may train them up in all holiness, and fit them for the enjoyment of God in all eternity." If God desires to glory in our children, I wonder, is He receiving glory in the way we parent them?

Nothing else we do as parents will have any eternal value unless we teach them the truth of God's Word. Moses said to put it in their hearts, their hands, their heads, and their homes (Deuteronomy 6). The psalmist said, "We will not hide them from the children" (Psalm 78:4). John said, "I have no greater joy than to hear that my children walk in truth" (3 John 1:4). The only way we will see them walking in truth when they are older is if they have seen us walking in truth when they were younger.

Truth is more easily communicated and received through a healthy, honest, and transparent relationship. We are discipling our children daily. Jesus said to his disciples, "If ye love me, keep my commandments." The willingness of the disciples to hear, receive and walk in truth was motivated by their relationship with the Savior. If all our children have after eighteen years is just a long list of rules, we have missed the point. We are molding them into the image of Christ by modeling before them the love of Christ. Don't leave them trapped in the unfinished work of your labor.

TAKEAWAYS:

- God entrusts parents to mold the faith of His children.
- Our motivation for parenting is to glorify God.
- We teach our children truth by modeling and living out truth before them in an honest and healthy relationship.

QUESTIONS:

What do you believe is the main objective of parenting?

_____

_____

_____

_____

_____

What unique challenges do children of ministers experience?

_____

_____

_____

_____

_____

List specific ways to model the truth before your children:

_____

_____

_____

_____

_____

PRAYER:

Dear Father, Your Word tells me that children are a heritage from the Lord. I realize that You have given me the opportunity to guide their lives and mold their identity. Help me to live in such a way that they will follow in Your steps and walk in Your truth. Guard their hearts, protect their minds, and bring Your joy into their lives.

44

FRIENDS IN THE FAITH

Selected Reading:

Ruth 1, Proverbs 27, John 15

"I would rather walk with a friend in the dark,
than alone in the light." –Helen Keller

S erving the Lord can be lonely at times. When Ahab and Jezebel threatened Elijah, he isolated himself in a cave. In the final moments of his life, the apostle Paul felt abandoned by all men. Daniel had no human contact in the lion's den. John the Revelator was exiled on the isle of Patmos. Even Jesus found himself without a prayer partner in the Garden of Gethsemane. I repeat: Serving the Lord can be lonely at times.

The ministry is unlike any vocation in the world; although we are surrounded by hundreds if not thousands of people, it is still possible to feel lonely without many friends. Those whom we minister to typically consider us to be shepherds, counselors, advisors, confidants, healers, teachers, and problem-solvers. The leadership role of the minister normally supersedes the friendship role thus leaving the true components of friendship at bay. This leaves the minister of God with many good, strong relationships, but with very few authentic friendships. Let me ask you a personal question: How many friends do you have?

Before you check your list on social media, let me rephrase the question: How many *real* friends do you have? The list probably just got smaller. Before you finalize those numbers, let us try one more question: How many *real* friends do you have that consider *you* a friend?

Charles Spurgeon said, "Friendship is one of the sweetest joys of life. Many might have failed beneath the bitterness of their trial had they not found a friend." It is true, every servant of God needs a few friends to help bear the load of ministry; but the number of authentic friends that you have is in direct relation to the number of people you have befriended. "A man that hath friends must shew himself friendly:" (Proverbs 18:24).

Healthy and honest friendships are built upon your investment, your interest, and your involvement in other people's lives and ministries. "You can make more friends in two months," said Dale Carnegie, "by becoming interested in other people than you can in two years by trying to get other people interested in you." How many friends do you have? That question can be answered by another: How often do you show yourself a friend?

TAKEAWAYS:

- It is possible to experience loneliness in the ministry.
- One can have many relationships but few friendships.
- To have a friend one must intentionally invest in others.

QUESTIONS:

If you had to compile a list of "real friends," who would be on it?

_____

_____

_____

_____

_____

Do you feel that you are friends with those you minister to?

_____

_____

_____

_____

_____

How do you invest in the friendships you have been given?

_____

_____

_____

_____

_____

PRAYER:

Dear Lord, thank You for the friends You have given me down through the years. I pray that You will bless their ministries, encourage their hearts, strengthen their families, and multiply their fruit. Help me to love them more, encourage them regularly, and befriend them often. Amen.

45

REMEMBER: YOU'RE A MEMBER

Selected Reading:

Matthew 16:13-20, Acts 2, 1 Corinthians 12

"A true Christian will find a body of believers somewhere,
*join himself to it and identify himself with it." --*A.W. Tozer

I am going to make an obvious statement that is not often a consideration in the life of the minister. Ready for it? Here it is: You are a member of your local church. I know, it is not the most theologically astounding observation you have ever heard. However, practically speaking, I think we often forget that we are an actual member of the church in which we serve.

If you are like me, much of your energy is focused upon serving others who come to the church service. Such concentration has biblical precedent. We are shepherds, teachers, and leaders who are obligated to "take the oversight" and "feed the flock of God." I do think, though, there's a temptation to view ourselves as the ones designated to "put on the show" for the others. I am not suggesting that we "perform" or "entertain" from week to week, but there is a pressure placed upon the minister of God to prepare and make ready the atmosphere and culture of worship in the local assembly. With such responsibility we must remember this fundamental truth: We are not only *ministers of the Body*; we are *members in the Body.*

God has placed you in a local church not only to feed others but to be fed, not only to administer spiritual gifts but to have gifts administered unto you, not only to evoke worship but to also engage in worship. The "come and see" atmosphere of the modern church puts an unbiblical strain upon the minister to outdo last week's performance. But the truth is, you are not an outsider whom others watch, you are organically placed inside the Body as a member situated for the glory of God (1 Corinthians 12:18).

Jesus will build His church and one day God will "present it to himself a glorious church, not having spot or wrinkle, or any such thing' (Ephesians 5:27). You are part of that divine institution. Every now and then it is good to look around the local assembly and realize that you have not been hired to entertain the sheep, you have been redeemed to glorify Christ as the Head. "Now ye are the body of Christ, and members in particular" (1 Corinthians 12:27).

TAKEAWAYS:

- Because of the constraints of the ministry, the minister of God can overlook his role as a church member.
- The Body of Christ is designed to help each member function in relation to one another.
- God has called us to be part *of* the church, not performers *for* the church. If we fail to see ourselves as members, we may fall into the trap of putting on a show for onlookers.

QUESTIONS:

How do you connect your leadership role with your membership?

_____

_____

_____

_____

_____

Is it difficult to worship during the church service? If so, why?

_____

_____

_____

_____

_____

In all honesty, do you feel the pressure to perform each week?

_____

_____

_____

_____

_____

PRAYER:

Holy God, what a joy it is to be part of the local church. Too often I approach worship with unnecessary and self-imposed pressure to create an experience for others. But Father, show me that I am part of the Body and that I need the church equally as much as the church needs me.

46

THE PEOPLE OF HIS PASTURE

Selected Reading:

Psalm 23, Jeremiah 25, 1 Peter 5

*"But when he saw the multitude, he was moved
with compassion on them."* –Matthew 9:36

No matter what facet of ministry you may be involved with, the fundamental component of that ministry is to serve other people. Whether you are preparing a lesson, studying for a sermon, cleaning a toilet, driving a church van, running the sound system, or opening the sanctuary door...at the heart of that service is the call to assist and help people.

People. When God calls a man to a certain location, He is calling that man to a community of people. This is the divine operation. God does not leave His people without pastoral care. He does not leave His flock unattended. It has jokingly been said that ministry would be easy if it were not for the people. But the truth is, if it were not for the people, there would be no ministry. In his book, *Spiritual Leadership,* Oswald Sanders points out this truth:

"A shepherd's work requires a shepherd's heart. The people we have to serve in the church or anywhere else are our special allotment; and our whole attitude to them must be the attitude of God; we must shepherd them like God. It is our task to show people the forbearance of God, the forgiveness of God, and the seeking love of God, the limitless service of God."

If the minister does not carefully guard his priorities, he may inadvertently overlook the congregation while being overloaded with his "to-do" list. No matter what the size, no matter where the geographical location, no matter how difficult the task, it is a divine honor for God's shepherds to superintend God's flock. This is his "special allotment." Therefore, we must love them, nurture them, exhort them, encourage them, guide them, and lead them to the True Shepherd and Bishop of their souls.

Take inventory of your congregation (whatever kind it may be), pray for them faithfully, exhort them to holiness, guide them with truth, call them by name, love them as a shepherd. God has not entrusted you with a program, He has called you to a people. Not just any people, but the people of God.

TAKEAWAYS:

- The ministry involves many components of service, but none more important than caring for the people of God.
- When God calls us to a certain location, He is calling us to the people in that community.
- God has not called us to a building but to a people.

QUESTIONS:

Do you view people as an interruption to your ministry? Explain.

_____

_____

_____

_____

_____

In what ways do you interact with those entrusted to your care?

_____

_____

_____

_____

_____

What would others say is your primary area of ministry?

_____

_____

_____

_____

_____

PRAYER:

Holy God, today I want to take some time to earnestly pray for the flock You have entrusted to my care. Their problems are big, their frustrations are many, their hearts are overwhelmed. Guide me to guide them to You. Help me not to be so encumbered with the tasks of ministry that I forget about the true meaning of ministry: Serving and loving others.

47

LEADING THE LEADERS

Selected Reading:
Exodus 17:8-16, Mark 9:1-8, 2 Timothy 2:1-3

*"Leadership that is entirely self-directed
will always be pathological."* –Mel Lawrenz

S everal years ago, I was privileged to have lunch with best-selling Christian author Stan Toler. Through some mutual friends, we met at a local Atlanta restaurant and discussed faith, family, life, and leadership. Mr. Toler, who has since passed, asked me about the various components of my ministry. As we discussed the challenge of my church's recent growth, he made this statement to me: You've got to lead *leaders* to lead *others*.

Though short and pithy, this simple maxim opened my heart to the biblical responsibility of equipping and training leaders around and within my ministry. Mr. Toler reiterated to me over lunch what he had written in his book, *Five-Star Church*, "The greatest asset in any congregation is its people and training your leaders will only enhance that asset."

This was the model of Jesus. Though He fed the thousands, and had one hundred and twenty people gathered in private prayer on

Pentecost, and though he called twelve men to be His disciples, when it came to His inner-circle, only Peter, James, and John made the list. Throughout His ministry, He would call those three men aside to teach and train them so that one day they would be able to teach and train His church.

You may not have a robust staff of full-time clergymen in your ministry, but you do have the responsibility to lead the leaders around you. A man who will not train others to help bear the load of leadership will not only face inevitable burn-out, he will also forfeit the joy of having multiplied fruit. He will limit his capacity to influence, he will impede the growth of his congregation, and he will become increasingly frustrated in the process.

Oftentimes we allow pride, insecurity, inability, or personal conflicts as excuses not to train those around us. As a result, we end up doing everything ourselves because "if you want it done right..." well, you know the rest.

But instead of trying to do everything yourself, it may be time to start leading the leaders *around* you so they can help you lead others *before* you. Take some time to evaluate your leadership team, your staff, your assistants, etc. Begin pouring into their lives and watch God do the work of overflow in others.

TAKEAWAYS:

- Leaders need to lead leaders so that they can lead others.
- The leader who refuses to train and equip others will eventually face burn-out in the ministry.
- Investing in others will lead to fruitful dividends.

QUESTIONS:

List the names of individuals whom you consider to be your leaders:

_____

_____

_____

_____

_____

Do you struggle to delegate responsibility? If so, why?

_____

_____

_____

_____

_____

How do you measure spiritual growth in your leadership team?

_____

_____

_____

_____

_____

PRAYER:

Dear Lord, There are so many responsibilities in the ministry. I must admit, sometimes I feel like I must take care of everything. Give me discernment to know who should be doing what. Equally, give me wisdom to train others around me to help bear the load so that You may receive maximum glory.

48

DISCIPLING THE FOLLOWERS

Selected Reading:

Mathew 28:16-20, Acts 2:38-47

"Those who teach by their doctrine
*must teach by their lives." –*Matthew Henry

T he data surrounding church attendance in this generation is pretty alarming on all fronts. The CCES Research Group has reported that in the past five years, eighteen percent of the population has left their religious affiliations, labeling themselves as either "non-religious" or "non-believers."

According to the Pew Research Group and the Lifeway Research Center, sixty-six percent of young people between the ages of 18-22 drop out of church every single year. That is a staggering number when you consider that this demographic is the second largest in the nation, just slightly behind the Baby Boomers (62 million millennials versus 70 million Baby Boomers).

In the millennial group, the study reveals an increasing acceptance of socialistic, atheistic, and agnostic philosophies. Seventy percent of that demographic will come to reject the traditional teachings of the church in which they were raised.

Why are we losing this generation? One could easily point to the ungodly influences of the world. We could certainly lay blame at the feet of liberal educators who intentionally indoctrinate their students with anti-God sentiments. Perhaps we could even point our fingers at liberal politicians who push their socialistic agendas down our throats. But at some point, the church must look at itself and take responsibility of the kind of fruit it is producing.

The church has been commissioned by Jesus Christ to make disciples; but unfortunately, those who leave the church never considered themselves as such. The church must get back to teaching and training its converts. If we fail to instruct followers to take up a cross, deny self, and walk with Christ, we should not be shocked when they walk away in another direction.

The minister of God should never dismiss the importance of maintaining a community of disciple-making. Yes, we should lead our leaders and pour into their lives, but we also need to surround ourselves with new converts and help them grow in their faith. When the church abandons its call for discipleship, it ultimately forfeits its right to be called a church. I would submit the same is true for the minister of God. In our fleshly efforts to grow the church, we rarely develop strong disciples, but if we sincerely desire to grow disciples, God will inevitably build His church.

TAKEAWAYS:

- Lack of discipleship leads to immature believers.
- Discipleship is the primary call of the Great Commission.
- The minister of God must personally disciple others.

QUESTIONS:

What is the main objective of the Great Commission? Explain below:

_____

_____

_____

_____

_____

Are you personally discipling anyone at this present time?

_____

_____

_____

_____

_____

Do you believe you have a discipleship environment in your church?

_____

_____

_____

_____

_____

PRAYER:

Heavenly Father, I turn to You with a heavy heart. There is such a spirit of confusion in these last days. This generation is being misled by so many ungodly influences. I pray that I will stand in the gap for them, reach out to them in love and make disciples of all nations. Give me the power of the Holy Spirit to do that which You have called me to do.

49

OUTSIDE THE WALLS

Selected Reading:
Acts 11:19-30, 1 Thessalonians 1, James 2:14-26

"It is the duty of every Christian to be
*Christ to his neighbor." –*Martin Luther

Years ago, a man knocked on my front door and presented a religious questionnaire to me and my family. He asked a variety of questions regarding my preferences of church culture. Do you like this kind of church or that kind of church? Do you prefer this kind of music or that kind of music? Do you lean toward this style of preaching or that style of preaching? He concluded his questioning by telling us that he was starting a ministry down the road and wanted to build a church in accordance with the likes and dislikes of the community.

This pragmatic approach to ministry was popular during the "seeker-sensitive" movement in days gone by. The idea was to build a church culture based upon the qualms and quirks of the community. This approach to church growth is an unbiblical method based upon carnal and shallow philosophy. The church should not be formed nor fashioned by the unregenerate preferences of the individuals in the community. Rather, as salt and light, the church has been charged with the responsibility to penetrate the culture with holy light, spiritual power, and life-changing truth. If a church tries to conform to the community, it will never see the community conform to the image of Christ.

However, the minister of God should not dismiss the relationship he has with the town or city in which he has been placed. He should wholly consider the responsibility that has been given to him as a gospel witness in his hometown. The Lord said to His disciples, "A city that is set on a hill cannot be hid…Let your light so shine before men, that they may see your good works, and glorify your Father which is in heaven" (Matthew 5:14-16). Paul told Timothy that a bishop must "have a good report of them which are without; let he fall into the reproach and the snare of the devil" (1 Timothy 3:7).

Your visibility, character, and reputation outside the walls of your church is the conduit in which the onlookers hear the gospel of Christ. God has called you and your church to be the watchers on the wall, the voice in the wilderness, the preserving salt of the earth and the penetrating light of the world. Glorify God in the community and the Lord will draw the community to Himself.

TAKEAWAYS:

- The community should not control the church's culture.
- The minister of God must guard his testimony with the community for the sake of the gospel.
- Passion for God leads to compassion for others.

QUESTIONS:

Does the community at large recognize the ministry of your church?

_____

_____

_____

_____

_____

In what ways do you connect with the surrounding culture?

_____

_____

_____

_____

_____

Do you study the demographics of your community? If so, explain:

_____

_____

_____

_____

_____

PRAYER:

Holy God, I come to You today with a burden to see my hometown saved by Your marvelous grace. Help me to be passionate for You so that I may be compassionate towards them. Help me to maintain a reputation of integrity so that the gospel of Jesus Christ can clearly be heard through my life. Amen.

50

TO REGIONS BEYOND

Selected Reading:
Mark 16:14-18, 1 Corinthians 2, Revelation 7

*"That they may rest from their labors; and their
works do follow them."* –Revelation 14:13

Just hours before His arrest and betrayal, Jesus prayed earnestly for His disciples regarding their position in the world. Even though they were "in this world" they were not "of this world." They had been called "out of this world," but Jesus in His final commission would send them "into this world" so that the world, through the preaching of the gospel could be saved. Jesus lovingly prayed, "As thou hast sent me into the world, even so have I also sent them into the world" (John 17:18).

The Father not only heard the high-priestly prayer of His Son, but He answered it through the world-changing preaching and teaching of the apostles. According to the citizens of Thessalonica, these were the ones who "turned the world upside down." They not only changed the religious, social, and cultural landscape of their day, but their witness for Christ had a world-wide impact on continents, concepts, and communities for generations to come.

It's hard to imagine that any one individual could have such a dramatic and longstanding effect on the entire world, but that is exactly what Christ had in mind when He said, "Go ye into the world and preach the gospel to every creature." As ministers of the gospel, we balance the tension of being *in* the world but not *of* the world; of being called *out* of the world but being called *into* the world. When we can situate those positions in proper alignment, God, in turn, uses our witness, our words, our worship, and our willingness to change our circles of influence thus causing global transformation. It may sound like a spiritual cliché, but it is true: You can change the world.

When a man begins influencing those around him with the gospel, the gospel in turn, begins reaching other people and places that the man could never physically reach or go himself. Take inventory, therefore, of your resources, your spiritual gifts, your networking, your friendships and evaluate how you are using them to advance the gospel. When it is all said and done, the world is the largest community in which you live. What are you doing to reach the regions beyond your hometown?

TAKEAWAYS:

- God calls us out of the world so that through our changed lives, He may use us in the world.
- The power of the gospel combined with the spiritual influence of the minister can have global effects.
- It is the responsibility of every minister to reach the world.

QUESTIONS:

Explain what it means to be called "out of" and "into" the world.

_____

_____

_____

_____

_____

Do you believe your ministry is making a global impact? If so, how?

_____

_____

_____

_____

_____

What relationships do you have with others in foreign fields?

_____

_____

_____

_____

_____

PRAYER:

Gracious Lord, As I approach Your throne, I thank You for calling me out of this world of darkness and into the kingdom of Your marvelous light. Help me to make changes in my life so that You can use me to make changes in Your world. Cause me to see the need for the preaching of the gospel to regions beyond. Amen.

PART 6:
THE CONFLICTS
OF THE MINISTER

51

DEALING WITH DOUBT

Selected Reading:
Genesis 17:15-21, Psalm 40, John 20:24-31

*"There was a castle called Doubting Castle,
the owner thereof was Giant Despair."* –John Bunyon

Out of all the conflicts the minister of God faces, doubt, perhaps is the most insidious. It not only calls into question the promises of God, but it gives way for the enemy to supplant truth with error, confirmation with confusion, and blessing with malice. Doubt, though small as a pebble, has slain many spiritual giants. Charles Spurgeon said:

> Some of us who have preached the Word for years, and have been the means of working faith in others and of establishing them in the knowledge of the fundamental doctrines of the Bible, have nevertheless been the subjects of the most fearful and violent doubts as to the truth of the very gospel we have preached.

Consider Thomas, who for three years was personally discipled by the Master Teacher but refused to believe in the resurrection of Christ until he had conclusive evidence. Or what about John the

Baptist, who heard the voice of the Father, saw the descension of the Spirit, and immersed the Lamb of God in the Jordan River. When cast into prison, he questioned whether Jesus was the Christ of Israel. How about Gideon who doubted the Lord's ability to use someone from such an insignificant family background. Or Sarah whose doubt caused her to laugh at the very notion she would ever have a child.

I would suggest that we are all, as Spurgeon said, "subjects of the most fearful and violent doubts." We are like the man whose child was tormented with an unclean spirit; we have enough faith to come to Christ and make our request known. But abiding somewhere in the shadows of uncertainty, we say, "I believe; help thou mine unbelief" (Mark 9:24).

Doubt is not the act of defiance. We should not confuse doubt as the operation of mistrusting God's Person or ability. When we doubt, we are not really asking the question "Can God do this?" rather we are wondering "Will God do this?"

It is imperative that a minster cling to truth even if he does not understand it. He must claim God's promises, even if he does not comprehend them. Is there uncertainty? Perhaps. But there is also faith, and wherever you find the smallest amount of faith, you will discover the ability to move the largest mountains of doubt.

TAKEAWAYS:

- Doubt hinders my ability to fully trust in God's promises.
- Some of the most faithful individuals experience doubt.
- Doubt is ultimately defeated by the power of faith.

QUESTIONS:

In your opinion, what's the difference between doubt and unbelief?

_____

_____

_____

_____

_____

In what area of your life do you experience the most doubt?

_____

_____

_____

_____

_____

How does Scripture enable you to overcome moments of doubt?

_____

_____

_____

_____

_____

PRAYER:

Mighty God, as I seek Your face today, I ask You to help mine unbelief. Lord, I know that You are all-powerful. I know that You are good. I know that You work all things for good in my life. However, sometimes in my weakness, I have doubts. Give me insight into Your Word, illuminate my mind with the power of Scripture and give me faith to believe.

52

CONFRONTING CRITICISM

Selected Reading:
1 Samuel 1, Nehemiah 6, Matthew 26:1-5

"I have derived continued criticism at all periods of my life, and do not remember any time when I was short of it." –Winston Churchill

C riticism is like a shot in the arm: It hurts but it eventually helps. To think you are above it is folly. To think you do not need it is arrogance. The reason we find criticism so difficult to deal with is because it touches the area of our heart that is often guarded and relentlessly defended: Pride. We may never admit it, but failure to embrace criticism is an attempt to claim perfection.

Granted, not all criticism is substantiated, warranted, or deserved; but our response to criticism is often the measuring rod of our character. Knowing that all men, especially those in the ministry, will face criticism, how do we biblically respond when we are raked over the proverbial coals?

We use it. If you are fortunate enough to have a friend who will look beyond your sensitivity and try to help you even when it hurts, then you should, with confidence, call that man a friend indeed. As a minister you will have to determine which critics are there to hurt you and which critics have been directed by God to help you. Examine your motives and determine whether there is merit in what has been said. If there is, repent and change.

We Refuse It. When I say "refuse it" I mean to ignore it, leave it alone, get over it. Break free from the bondage of man's judgment. Find contentment in Christ. One of the mistakes we oftentimes make in ministry is to fulfill everyone's expectations of what they think we should be, all the while, we come short of pleasing the One Who matters the most: God. Refuse to live in the shadow of the pointed finger.

We Defuse It. Criticism can be defused through confrontation. When we take biblical steps toward reconciliation, God imparts to us a sense of liberty. Admittedly, there are some critics you will never be able to come to terms with, but when possible, approach the cynics of life with a desire to resolve contention. The one thing we must avoid is trying to avoid criticism altogether. Not all criticism is bad. As a matter of fact, there are times when it is necessary. When given in the right spirit, with the right motive, under the right circumstances, criticism can be your greatest companion. "Faithful are the wounds of a friend" (Proverbs 27:6).

TAKEAWAYS:

- No one is exempt from criticism. Even Christ had critics.
- We can either use, refuse, or defuse criticism.
- Criticism, though hurtful, can help us grow in our ministries, our reputation, and our faith.

QUESTIONS:

List some situations where you have dealt with criticism.

_____

_____

_____

_____

_____

How did you respond when faced with criticism?

_____

_____

_____

_____

_____

What specifically have you learned from such conflicts?

_____

_____

_____

_____

_____

PRAYER:

Dear Lord, I realize I am not above criticism. You were criticized continually by the religious system during Your earthly ministry. I know You understand what my heart and mind feel like during such moments. Help me to use the criticism to become a more effective leader and minster of the gospel.

53

SPIRITUAL OPPRESSION

Selected Reading:

Exodus 2, 1 Samuel 17, 2 Kings 10

"If God were not my friend, Satan would
not so much be my enemy." –Thomas Brooks

In his letters to Timothy, Paul used military language to convey the reality of the spiritual battles he would encounter in the work of the Lord. He told his young son to "be strong in the grace that is in Christ Jesus" and to "endure hardness, as a good soldier of Jesus Christ" that he may "please him who hath chosen him to be a soldier" (1 Timothy 2:1,3,4). Timothy was the pastor of the Ephesian church, and it was to this congregation the apostle exhorted, "Put on the whole armor of God, that ye may be able to stand against the wiles of the devil" (Ephesians 6:11).

Timothy experienced many difficulties in the ministry. From dealing with false teachers to validating his maturity among the congregation to defending the imprisonment of his mentor; Timothy knew what it was like to face ministerial struggles. But out of all the difficulties he encountered none was more oppressive than the spiritual attacks from the enemy. If Timothy would survive, he would have to learn to fight like a soldier in the army, the reason being: The ministry, at times, is a warzone.

Because the Holy Spirit abides within, the true believer never faces the possibility of being *possessed* by the enemy; however, that does not stop the adversary from doing all he can to *oppress* the believer. Spiritual oppression is the act whereby the enemy does all he can to manipulate and distort truth in the mind and heart of the minister through waves of deception and lies. It would be much easier to "wrestle with flesh and blood" in the physical realm than to face the unpredicted, out-of-nowhere assaults administered in those dark seasons. The objective is to hold the minister of God as a hostage in the prisons of despair, confusion, and hopelessness. The enemy's desire is to remove you from the frontlines of the battle so that you are no longer a threat.

It is only through prayer and the Word of God that we can overcome spiritual oppression. Prayer is the channel in which we communicate with the Heavenly Captain, and Scripture is the provided weapon that allows us to combat the enemy's lies. To overcome we must put on the "whole armor of God," take a stand in the face of the adversary, pray to the Lord of heaven, and use God's Word as a means of defense. "Submit yourselves therefore to God. Resist the devil, and he will flee from you" (James 4:7).

TAKEAWAYS:

- Oppression is the manipulation of truth in our minds.
- Those who stand on the frontlines are subject to attack.
- Prayer and Scripture help secure victory over oppression.

QUESTIONS:

What words would you use to describe spiritual oppression?

_____

_____

_____

_____

_____

How has the enemy specifically attacked your mind and heart?

_____

_____

_____

_____

_____

What verses can you use to overcome moments of oppression?

_____

_____

_____

_____

_____

PRAYER:

Dear Father, You are my Captain, You are my hightower, my refuge, my shield. Give me discernment to know when I am being assaulted by the enemy. Give me spiritual power to overcome through prayer and Scripture. I submit my life to you and resist the devil in Your holy name.

54

EMOTIONAL DEPRESSION

Selected Reading:

1 Samuel 30:1-7, Job 2, Psalm 124

"Fits of depression come over
the most of us." –Charles Spurgeon

Aording to the Britannica dictionary, the word depression is a "mood or state marked by feelings of low self-worth and/or guilt; it is a reduced ability to enjoy life." No matter what set of statistics you look at these days, you will discover this one solemn truth: Our generation is down in the dumps. The mental health data for those who serve in the ministry does not fare any better than those who sit in the pews.

In 2019, Lifeway Research Group reported that nearly twenty-five percent of senior pastors deal with some form of depression/anxiety on a regular basis. This is the same number among all adults in America. The same study also revealed that most pastors frequently contemplate quitting, they deal with disappointment on a weekly basis, and many times feel ill-prepared for the complex situations they encounter in the ministry. Perhaps most discouraging, they feel as though they have no one to talk with about their emotional or spiritual state. This "reduces their ability to enjoy life" leaving them (us) with feelings of depression. The minister of God may experience depression for a variety of reasons: Unfair expectations, low self-worth, spiritual warfare, lack of support, overexposure to death and sickness, secret sin, the burdens and weights of his parishioners, uncertainty about the future…and the list goes on and on.

We do not need any more reasons to be depressed, instead, we need to be like King David and learn to "encourage ourselves in the Lord." If anyone knew about depression, stress, and emotional anxiety, it was Jesse's youngest son. One only need to read through a few of his psalms to discover his emotional state was not always upbeat and positive. But David did know the Lord, and he did know something about getting in the secret place under the shadowy wings of the Almighty. He knew *where to go* when he had no idea *what to do.*

The minister of God must find his true contentment in Christ. When life sends you down to the lowlands of despair and you cannot see the light of day, it is there you must recognize your true identity in Jesus. He is your light and salvation. He loves you and joyfully calls you to Himself. Embrace His tender passion, accept His grace, and rest awhile in the green pastures of His care.

TAKEAWAYS:

- Ministers are not exempt from depression or anxiety.
- At times it can feel as though we are facing life alone.
- True joy is discovered through our identity in Jesus Christ.

QUESTIONS:

How does depression or anxiety manifest itself in your life?

_____

_____

_____

_____

_____

In those moments, do you have certain people you can talk with?

_____

_____

_____

_____

_____

Is it possible to thwart off depression before it happens? If so, how?

_____

_____

_____

_____

_____

PRAYER:

Dear God, in moments of despair, help me to see my true worth, my true self, my true identity in You. Many times, I allow external situations to dictate and control my attitude and mindset. Give me grace to look toward You, the Shepherd of my valley, the Refuge in my storm. Hide me in the secret place until I can find the joy of the Lord. Amen.

55

THE AILMENT OF APATHY

Selected Reading:
Numbers 14:1-10, Ecclesiastes 1, Jonah 4

*"All growth that is not toward God
is going to decay."* –George MacDonald

Apathy is a cancer in the body of the church. It may be discovered in one isolated area, but rarely is it confined to that location. It has the potential to spread to the other members until the entire congregation becomes diseased with indifference. The fastest-growing form of this infection is the kind that develops in the minister of God. If he becomes indifferent to the work of the Lord, it will not take long until the entire operation is on life-support. If apathy is a potential cancer in the service of the Lord, how do we cut it out?

Through Intentionality. Believers fail to succeed at spiritual victories because somewhere in their minds they never intend to gain them. Say what you will, people do what they *want* to do because they *intend* to do it. If a believer is going to thrive in his walk with Christ, he must be deliberate. He must set goals, make up his mind, rely on the Spirit, and intentionally seek the Lord.

Through Inspiration. The apathetic life is rarely stimulated by the beauty and awe of God. To circumvent such disquieted living, you must be willing to see the sovereign enterprise all around you. Take a walk, read a book, watch a movie, explore the world. Stop, look around, look up, and discover anew the majesty of God.

Through Influences. A life becomes cold and hardened when it fails to be touched by the warmth of others. To safeguard yourself from apathy, seek the influence of those who live for God, who grow in grace, who pursue the kingdom. Spend some time near their fire; see if it does not stir the embers of your heart.

Through Intercession. Pray breeds devotion. Pray births delight. Prayer brings determination. When someone frequently engages their heart and mind in the act of prayer, they will be more inclined to keep their eyes and affections on the eternal. The greatest position in overcoming apathy is the one on your knees.

Through Increase. Apathy says, "I have all I need, all I want, all I desire to know." Apathetic people, in a very real sense, have already come to the end of their lives, they have accepted their cancer. To that end I implore you: Treatment cannot be prolonged! Divine consultation is needed today! Find a place at the feet of the Great Physician and let Him treat the ailment of apathy.

TAKEAWAYS:

- Apathy in the ministry can be contagious to others.
- We must intentionally seek the right kind of influences and inspiration to combat apathetic living.
- At times we need to repent of the indifference in our lives.

QUESTIONS:

How do you detect apathy in your life and ministry?

_____

_____

_____

_____

_____

What brings about the most joy in your life? The most frustrations?

_____

_____

_____

_____

_____

List specific things you can intentionally do to overcome apathy:

_____

_____

_____

_____

_____

PRAYER:

Dear Lord, Renew in my heart the joy of thy salvation. Guard my desires, keep my steps, and thrill my soul with Your presence. Help me not to become indifferent to serving You, to knowing You, to living for You. Direct my attention to areas in my ministry that need stirring and then by Your grace, stir the gift of God that is within me. Amen.

56

PURGING OUT PRIDE

Selected Reading:

Psalm 10, Proverbs 29, 1 John 2

"Pride gets no pleasure out of having something, only out of having more of it than the next man." –C.S. Lewis

P ride is an ironic altar where those who are consumed with glory bow down to themselves. It is there the parishioner trades his sacrifice, his humility, his service for a pompous seat upon an engraved throne of arrogance. I say "ironic" because at this shrine, the god *and* the worshipper are one and the same. Pride is idolatry in its purest form.

Pride begins with the act of making oneself a god; but never satisfied, it needs followers, it needs worshippers. Therefore, we outdo one another so that we can have a greater audience of praise. C.S. Lewis made this assessment years ago:

> "We say that people are proud of being rich, or clever, or good-looking, but they are not. They are proud of being richer, or cleverer, or better-looking than others. Nearly all those evils which people put down to greed or selfishness are really far more the result of pride."

At the core of every prideful act is the need to be praised. Therefore, we place ourselves in competitive scenarios so that when we win, we win with the hopes of receiving glory. Pride is not content with having something; its contentment is based upon having more than the next fellow down the road, the lady across the pew, or the ministry across town.

The only victory, the only triumph against this sinister force is the cross of Jesus Christ. The antithesis of pride is not necessarily humility, but rather sacrifice…death even. Christ made himself of "no reputation" and took upon him the form of a servant…and become obedient unto death, even the death of the cross.

Therefore, the sons of Adam will only find victory from pride in the Son of God, the second Adam. If we could humble ourselves enough, we would only be proud of it. Therefore, our victory from pride can only come through our righteous standing before God in Christ Jesus. It is His death that drives away the life force of pride. I have found it difficult in my own life to applaud myself while holding the rugged timbers of the cross. Therein is my victory from pride; it is there that God purges it from my life.

TAKEAWAYS:

- At its core, pride is nothing less that idolatry.
- Pride can manifest itself through competition with other ministries or other individuals.
- The remedy against pride is the cross of Jesus Christ. His example of humility reminds us that we have been called to serve others.

QUESTIONS:

How does pride manifest itself in your ministry?

_____

_____

_____

_____

_____

Is there a difference between being proud and being prideful?

_____

_____

_____

_____

_____

How does the cross of Christ purge pride from our hearts?

_____

_____

_____

_____

_____

PRAYER:

Heavenly Father, Search my heart for pride. Purge it with the divine power of Your Holy Spirit. Help me to see the example You left behind as a Servant. Help me to grab the towel of humility and realize that my position before the throne is only merited by grace, and Your grace alone. There is no good thing in me outside of Your abiding Spirit. Amen.

57

THE WEARINESS OF WAITING

Selected Reading:
Genesis 37, Psalm 25, Psalm 62

*"If you do not know what to do,
stand still until you do."* –F.B. Meyer

Difficulty in life is not the *real* difficulty. It is the uncertainty of time associated with the difficulty that really troubles us. If you know you are going to wait at the doctor's office for an extra twenty minutes, you may not like it, but you accept it. However, if you wait without anyone communicating to you that it will take an extra twenty minutes...well, now, that's the issue, isn't it? It is time, really, and all its extended uncertainties that cause us to be anxious.

Waiting is the hardest bunch of nothing that I've ever had to do. Now, that may sound confusing and grammatically incorrect, but it is true. Waiting is tough, and seemingly useless. If it were up to me and you, we would never wait. All would be perfect if we could exempt ourselves from the waiting lines of life. The only problem with such plausible thinking is that it foolishly places our will above the will of God. He has orchestrated life with velvety ropes, and sometimes the line is long. Longer than we can even imagine. The very idea of waiting on God is an affirmation of your need and dependency upon Him. The Bible says, "They that wait upon the Lord shall renew their strength." We are not waiting on ourselves, because if we could resolve the issues in our own power, we would do it quickly. Rather, we are waiting on God, and in waiting on God, we recognize His authority in our lives.

The very concept and idea of waiting is a concept of authority. You wait because someone or something is controlling the time. You wait at the red light because you recognize the moral law of the concept. You wait on test results because you recognize the advanced intelligence of the one administering the exam. You wait on God because, well, He is God, and He is above all and before all. His authority supersedes my impatience.

Therefore, God allows His children to wait so that when the strength is renewed, when the child is restored, when the bill is paid, when the home is repaired, when the mind is settled, when the job is secured, when the peace is felt, when the answers are provided, there will be no denying Him the glory. So, go ahead and wait, it may be awhile...but it's always worth it.

TAKEAWAYS:

- Man is an impatient creature, wanting to hurry God along.
- The issue of waiting is really an issue of accepting God's sovereignty in our lives.
- God develops our ministries through the crucible of time; therefore, we should trust Him in the process.

QUESTIONS:

What is the most difficult component of waiting on God?

_____

_____

_____

_____

_____

Are you waiting on God to do something in your ministry? Explain:

_____

_____

_____

_____

_____

How does God grow His ministers through the waiting process?

_____

_____

_____

_____

_____

PRAYER:

Dear God, I must confess that I find it difficult to wait. I am in a perpetual hurry and for whatever reason, I can be at odds with Your timing. Please forgive my impatience. I realize that life doesn't always unfold the way I anticipate. During those waiting seasons, please give me wings to rise, run, walk, and be renewed. Amen.

58

TROUBLED BY TEMPTATION

Selected Reading:
2 Samuel 11, Psalm 38, Acts 5:1-11

"What makes resisting temptation so difficult for many people is they don't want to discourage it completely." –Benjamin Franklin

When Jesus overcame the reptilian temptations in the desert, He did so with a precise and powerful unleashing of Scripture. Where Adam failed in every conceivable way in perfect paradise, Jesus rose victorious in the most inhospitable environments imaginable. Though Jesus had the ability to turn the stones into bread and satisfy the natural hunger of His humanity, He refused the invitation to such a meal. Adam chose fruit and was spiritually consumed in death. The Second Adam chose bread and was sustained in life.

Every hellish blow that was released by Satan was blocked by Holy revelation. In response to the devil's unqualified and unwarranted challenge, Jesus said, "Man shall not live by bread alone, but by every word that proceedeth out of the mouth of God" (Matthew 4:4). Jesus was not saying this for Himself, He was saying this for you. As a matter of fact, He was not being tempted to validate Himself to the devil; the adversary knew exactly Who Christ was, is, and will always be. Christ suffered in the howling wasteland so that you and I would be able to overcome our own temptations. He modeled the perfect example of the great need we all have in yielding to the Word of God for sustenance and life.

Jesus taught us that man lives by the Word of God, not just natural bread. Even as bread sustains and strengthens the natural body, the Word of God sustains and strengthens the spiritual man. But it must be consumed. Think about it, *eating* bread is not the same thing as *cooking* bread. The minister of God, in preparing the meal, must not dismiss his own need for digestion.

Jesus did not say to only *read* the Word, or *learn* the Word, or *memorize* the Word, or *quote* the Word, or *proclaim* the Word, or to *even know* the Word. He said to "live by the Word." Beloved, the only way to overcome temptation, rise above the enemy, yield to the Spirit's call, sustain the spiritual man, and have power to fulfill the assignment ahead is if you are daily consuming and living by the Word of God. "Any day we neglect to feed on the Word of God," said R.A. Torrey, "we leave an open door in which Satan is sure to enter our hearts and lives." Shut the door, grab some bread, and enjoy the meal.

TAKEAWAYS:

- When man refuses God's Word he falls into temptation.
- In Christ's temptation, He was providing an example for us to be able to overcome the enemy.
- The Word of God provides sustenance for the soul.

QUESTIONS:

Describe the correlation between victory over sin and Scripture.

_____

_____

_____

_____

_____

Where are you when you experience the most-heated temptation?

_____

_____

_____

_____

_____

Do you read and study Scripture outside of the context of ministry?

_____

_____

_____

_____

_____

PRAYER:

My Holy Savior, as I approach Your throne, I know that I have an advocate with the Father. Dear Lord, You are righteous, holy, and good. You have given me a way to flee temptation. Help me to call upon You in those moments when Satan tempts my soul. Let the Word of God be a shield for me. In Your name I pray, Amen.

59

TORN BY A THORN

Selected Reading:
Isaiah 38, James 1:1-6, 1 Peter 1:1-12

"Health is a good thing, but sickness is far better...
if it leads us to God." –J.C. Ryle

There is a brand of pop theology that promises freedom from poverty, suffering, and physical ailments. If you have enough faith, you will never be sick, you will never be financially downtrodden, and you will never experience pain. The major issue with this teaching is that, while it uses biblical language, it does not line up with actual biblical truth.

The reality is, sometimes God allows, even orchestrates situations where we experience physical pain. Consider the suffering of Job, or the man who was born blind for the glory of God, or the sickness and death of Lazarus. These individuals did not lack faith. Job was a righteous man. The blind man (nor his parents) had sinned. And Lazarus was a close friend to Jesus.

Consider Paul, who was a chosen apostle, a light to the Gentiles, a preacher of the gospel, a writer of Scripture, a builder of churches, a missionary to the nations, and a faithful servant of the Lord Jesus Christ. If anyone had faith it was Paul, yet he did not escape the physical calamities of living in a sin-cursed world. Paul detailed his physical suffering this way:

> "And lest I should be exalted above measure through the abundance of the revelations, there was given to me a thorn in the flesh, the messenger of Satan to buffet me, lest I should be exalted above measure. For this thing I besought the Lord thrice, that it might depart from me. And he said unto me, My grace is sufficient for thee: for my strength is made perfect in weakness" (2 Corinthians 12:7-9)

Physical sickness is not only a possibility in the ministry, it is a divine instrument used of God to bestow His strength. Paul's thorn may have torn his side for a season, but it simultaneously administered a measure of grace. Paul eventually came to view his physical suffering as a gift (there was *given* me a thorn). Through the thorn, pride was removed from his heart. Through the thorn, God brought Paul closer to Himself in prayer. Through the thorn, Paul experienced the sufficiency of grace. Sometimes, God's most benevolent gifts are wrapped in the packaging of sickness, suffering, and pain. Such sorrow draws us closer to the Physician.

TAKEAWAYS:

- Physical pain is part of the human experience, regardless of one's spirituality.
- In sickness, we must trust in the providential hand of God to provide grace and strength.
- "Thorns" are opportunities for others to see Christ in us.

QUESTIONS:

In your experience, describe the effect sickness has on faith.

_____

_____

_____

_____

_____

Why do you believe God allows sickness to enter our lives?

_____

_____

_____

_____

_____

Do you think sickness better equips you to serve others? If so, how?

_____

_____

_____

_____

_____

PRAYER:

Great Physician, I call upon Your name today realizing that You work all things for my good. Even in the pain and the suffering, I can sense the sufficiency of Your grace. Help me to use my adversities to better serve those who are under my care and leadership. Bring healing, restoration, and peace during the times of my life when I suffer physical pain.

60

THE BURDEN OF BITTERNESS

Selected Reading:

Job 23, Lamentations 3, Hebrews 12:12-17

"When you harbor bitterness, happiness will
dock somewhere else." –Anonymous

itter. It's hard to even say the word without puckering your lips. Go ahead, say it slowly. I suppose it is fitting that the pronunciation of the word should match its definition. Webster describes it as "a taste sensation that is peculiarly acrid, astringent, and disagreeable." In Scripture, bitter is translated from the Greek word *pikros*, which has an association with the taste of poison. The true danger in drinking poison is not really in the taste, but rather the effects it has once it is swallowed.

Metaphorically, and perhaps more frequently, it refers to the state of one's spirit when they have been treated unfairly. It speaks of "sharpness of soul" or literally, being hurt or cut to the bone.

Granted, it may be possible to execute responsibilities in the ministry when you have a bitter taste in your mouth; but I would contend that it is next to impossible to fulfill your assignment when you have bitterness down in the soul. Let us be honest, ministry can have some pretty sour moments. Just ask Joseph who was betrayed by his own brothers, or Hannah, who was ridiculed for her infertility, or Naomi who lost a husband and three sons in Moab, or Jeremiah who was incarcerated for declaring the oracles of God. Ministry without a little misery is a complete misnomer; however, if we allow those distasteful moments to occupy and control our lives, we will, over time become spiritually paralyzed. "This is what bitterness does," said John Courson, "it is like taking a bottle of poison, swallowing it, and waiting for the other person to die."

Bitterness that is buried in the soil of your heart, will eventually be detected in the pupil of your eye; you just cannot hide it. As vile as the root of bitterness is, the fruit is even worse. Bitterness leads to a ministry that is characterized by strife, jealousy, discontentment, hatred, delusion, spite, and joylessness.

The only way to uproot this putrid beast is to embrace the grace of God. Christ, our supreme example, drank the cup of our bitterness and willingly pardoned our transgressions. For those who have tasted the Lord and have experienced divine mercy, they must be willing to kill off bitterness with compassion and extend to others what they have graciously been granted: Forgiveness.

TAKEAWAYS:

- Bitterness is a danger to the soul.
- When I harbor bitterness in my life, it renders me ineffective in the service of the Lord.
- The only thing that will uproot bitterness is God's grace.

QUESTIONS:

List some causes of bitterness in the ministry.

_____

_____

_____

_____

_____

In your opinion, why is bitterness so difficult to uproot?

_____

_____

_____

_____

_____

How does bitterness with others affect our relationship with God?

_____

_____

_____

_____

_____

PRAYER:

Righteous Father, Help me not to become engrossed with a bitter spirit. When I experience hurt, betrayal, suffering, and wrongdoing from others, let me extend to them the same grace You have extended to me. If there is any bitterness in my heart, uproot it now by the power of the Holy Spirit, and plant within me the mercies of God anew. Amen.

PART 7:
THE CONSOLATION OF THE MINISTER

61

UNSPEAKABLE JOY

Selected Reading:
Nehemiah 8:10, Psalm 100, 1 Peter 4:13

"What starts out as hard doesn't remain hard when joy enters the process." –Bill Hull

In March of 1941, a young Jewish girl by the name of Etty Hillesum began writing in her diary about the experience she had in the concentration camps at Auschwitz. She witnessed the atrocious accounts of her countrymen dying in furnaces. She was subjected to the inhumane terror of Hitler and his tyrannical regime; yet somehow in the most diabolical of circumstances, she kept an "uninterrupted dialogue" with God. In one section of the diary she recorded:

"Sometimes when I stand in some corner of the camp, my feet planted on Your earth, my eyes raised towards Your heaven, tears sometimes run down my face, tears of deep emotion and gratitude. I want to be there right in the thick of what people call horror and still be able to say that life is beautiful. Yes, I lie in a corner, parched and dizzy and feverish and unable to do a thing. Yet I am also with the jasmine and the piece of sky beyond my window."

265

In his first epistle, the apostle Peter wrote to believers, who, much like Etty Hillesum, were experiencing the furnaces of faith. The early church fell under intense persecution at the hand of Nero and the Roman Empire. Their "fiery trials" included public beatings, imprisonment, torture, and execution. In response to the cultural antagonism, Peter reminded the church that in the midst of their "manifold temptations," they could have "joy unspeakable and full of glory" (1 Peter 1:8).

Ironic is this subject of joy, for it is often discovered when the furnace is heated to the highest degree. It is other-worldly, it resides in the bosom of Jesus Christ and only those who draw close to His side can taste of its spring. Jesus said, "These things have I spoken unto you, that my joy might remain in you, and that your joy might be full" (John 15:11). Therein, is the secret of unspeakable joy; it is only given to those who "abide" in the Lord.

Like Etty, and like the early church believers, when you find yourself in the presence of the Joy-Giver, when you lay your head upon His breast, there is an everlasting elation that overshadows the smoke and fire of the furnace. With feet planted on the earth, and eyes raised toward heaven, you can say, "For I reckon that the sufferings of this present time are not worthy to be compared with the glory which shall be revealed in us" (Romans 8:18). What joy!

TAKEAWAYS:

- Joy is often, and ironically, discovered in adversity.
- The promise of joy is given to those who abide in Christ.
- Perspective, not circumstance, is the means of having joy.

QUESTIONS:

Do you "count it all joy" when you fall into divers temptations?

_____

_____

_____

_____

_____

Do you believe your perspective influences your emotions? Explain.

_____

_____

_____

_____

_____

What did Jesus mean when He said that His joy would be in you?

_____

_____

_____

_____

_____

PRAYER:

Almighty God, You have designed joy in such a way that it can be discovered even in the most horrific of circumstances. When I keep my eyes on You, when I draw close to Your side, I find that Your joy is undeniable. Thank you for such a promise! Amen.

62

INDESCRIBABLE PEACE

Selected Reading:
Job 22:21, Isaiah 9:6, John 14

"The world can create trouble in peace, but God can create peace in trouble." –Thomas Watson

The book of Philippians is perhaps the most positive and uplifting epistle of the apostle Paul's writings. It contains some of the most inspiring verses for the Christian life. "For to me to live is Christ, and to die is gain" was Paul's theme. He genuinely wanted his fellow believers to "have the mind of Christ" and experience "the power of his resurrection, and the fellowship of his sufferings." Paul knew he "could do all things through Christ" and desired the same reality for those at Philippi.

Paul's optimistic outlook is encouraging, but what makes his words that much more inspiring is the fact that he penned them down in a Roman prison. Under house arrest, chained to a solider, betrayed by companions, hated by the world, with many scars and with much affliction, Paul assuredly spoke these words, "And the peace of God, which passeth all understanding, shall keep your hearts and minds through Christ Jesus" (Philippians 4:7).

269

Paul had peace. Not just any peace. Not the peace of the world. Not the peace of financial security. Not the peace of civil liberties. Not the peace of popular consent. No, his peace extended far beyond the tranquilities of the natural realm. His peace was divine; it was the peace *of* God. If permitted by the Holy Spirit, the apostle Paul would have gladly described this peace to his reader; however, its description was beyond comprehension. Literally, there were no words to explain its scope or grandiosity.

How does one experience this kind of peace? Paul said, "Be careful for nothing: but in every thing by prayer and supplication with thanksgiving let your requests be made known unto God." Prayer and praise are interchangeable with peace. They interlock in such an inexplicable way that you cannot tell where one ends and the other begins.

It is true, Paul faced a plethora of challenges throughout the course of his ministry. One only need to read through the outlined list of woes in 2 Corinthians 11 to discover Paul's ongoing trouble. But, in every peril, in every problem, in every prison, Paul bowed his heart in prayer and praise. His utter dependence upon God "in everything" gave way to a peace that was beyond comprehension. Such peace is still available today for those who labor in prayer.

TAKEAWAYS:

- Peace is not based upon external comfort or ease.
- Those who experience the peace of God will find themselves in a perpetual state of prayer.
- Peace can be fully experienced, but not fully described.

QUESTIONS:

Recall any difficult situations in which you experienced God's peace.

_____

_____

_____

_____

_____

Is there a difference in the peace *of* God and the peace *from* God?

_____

_____

_____

_____

_____

Explain the connection between prayer, praise, and peace.

_____

_____

_____

_____

_____

PRAYER:

Great God and Savior, To know that You are in control, and to know that You hold my life in Your hand, brings peace that cannot be discovered anywhere else. Help me to bring every matter, every situation to You in supplication. Through prayer and praise, give Your servant divine peace.

63

UNFATHOMABLE LOVE

Selected Reading:

John 13:23-35, 2 Corinthians 5:14

"God loves each of us as if there
were only one of us." –Augustine

One of the greatest prayers recorded in Scripture is found in the book of Ephesians. With bowed knees before the Father, the apostle Paul prayed for the church to have spiritual enlightenment regarding the love of Christ.

> "That Christ may dwell in your hearts by faith; that ye, being rooted and grounded in love, May be able to comprehend with all saints what is the breadth, and length, and depth, and height; And to know the love of Christ, which passeth knowledge, that ye might be filled with all the fullness of God" (Ephesians 3:17-19).

Paul said that the love of Christ "passeth knowledge;" but he also prayed for the saints to comprehend Christ's love. In other words, Paul was saying, "I'm praying that you will understand something that you will never fully understand." At first glance, that may sound contradictory, but the truth is, Paul was inviting them to embrace, engage, and enjoy the great dimensions of Christ's love. Specifically, he prayed for them to comprehend:

The expanse of Christ's love (breadth). It is so wide that it crosses the canyons of time and space. It reaches as far as east is to west, casting our sin away from the presence of God.

The eternality of Christ's love (length). How long will God's love last? Spurgeon said, "It is so long that your old age cannot wear it out, so long your continual tribulation cannot exhaust it, your successive failure and temptations cannot drain it; like eternity itself it knows no bounds."

The extent of Christ's love (depth). Like an ocean, we could never reach the bottom. It plunges deeper than our sin, lower than our depravity, and is more voluminous than all our transgressions.

The elevation of Christ's love (height). Up from the grave, up from our deadness, up from hell and up into glory, where we are seated in heavenly places with Christ Jesus!

The love of Christ "constraineth us." It is His love for me that compels me to serve others. If I minister from the vantage point of *my love* for Him, I will be limited to only serve some people, some places, and only sometimes. But if I minister out of *Christ's love* for me, I will be able to go into all the world, to all people at any time with the message of His glorious gospel!

TAKEAWAYS:

- Having God's fullness means understanding Christ's love.
- The depths of His love are greater than our knowledge.
- His love for me is the great motivation for my service.

QUESTIONS:

How can we better understand the love of Christ?

_____

_____

_____

_____

_____

What other verses describe the "dimensions" of God's love?

_____

_____

_____

_____

_____

How does your love for Christ, and His love for you intertwine?

_____

_____

_____

_____

_____

PRAYER:

Precious Lord, I pray You will give me a greater understanding of the vast dimensions of Your love. I also pray this prayer, as Paul did, for my family and friends, and for the people to whom I minister. Fill us with the fullness of God and let your love grow in all directions among us.

64

LIVELY HOPE

Selected Reading:
Psalm 33, Proverbs 10:28, Romans 5:1-5

"Never be afraid to trust an unknown future to a known God." –Corrie Ten Boom

In 2017, Ethan Siegel published an article in Forbes Magazine outlining his prediction of the world's demise. As a staunch advocate of global warming, Siegel believes the process is well underway. He described the development in four stages.

1. Through the evolutionary process, the sun is currently mutating and become more violent with each passing season.

2. This will inevitably have a warming and boiling effect on the oceans. He contends, "For billions of years, earth has been an ocean-covered world, with simple and complex life originating in the seas and only coming onto land relatively recently. Yet thanks to the evolution of our sun, our oceans won't be around forever."

3. With the oceans drying up, the planet will inevitably turn into a giant "ash heap." Evaporation will lead to starvation. Plant, animal, and human life will quickly fade away.

4. Finally, our corpse of a planet will swell to the point of explosion or be forced out of its orbit. The global chain reaction of such an event would lead to these final catastrophic possibilities:

- An object collides with the earth and destroys it.
- A massive object passes close by the earth, gravitationally ejecting it from the Solar System where it wanders in obscurity throughout the empty cosmos for eternity.
- Or it remains bound to the sun's corpse, and slowly, over countless orbits, spirals into our stellar remnant, where it's swallowed by whatever is left of our Solar System.

No matter how you look at Siegel's prediction, there is not much hope for mankind. The truth is, God will judge the planet in the tribulation and all the cosmos will fall underneath the weight of His final verdict. However, for the child of God, we have the hope of a new heaven and new earth.

To say that we have hope is to say that we have a desire to see a promised fulfilled. Furthermore, it is to trust in the moral character of the One making the promise. God has "begotten us again unto a lively hope by the resurrection of Jesus Christ from the dead, To an inheritance incorruptible, and undefiled, and that fadeth not away, reserved in heaven for you" (1 Peter 1:3-4). Our hope is not in the *sun* going away, it is in the *Son* coming back.

TAKEAWAYS:

- The world is looking for ways to explain cosmic groaning.
- Hope is an earnest expectation of a future event.
- The hope of the believer is made alive by Christ's return.

QUESTIONS:

How does the return of Jesus motivate you for ministry?

_____

_____

_____

_____

_____

Give a biblical definition of the word "hope."

_____

_____

_____

_____

_____

How does faith and hope relate to one another?

_____

_____

_____

_____

_____

PRAYER:

Coming King, You have not left us without a hope, a lively, living hope. I am glad that our hope is not in this life only, but we have the promise of eternal redemption with You in heaven. May Your return give me the hope I need to look for You and to labor for souls until You come.

65

VICTORIOUS FAITH

Selected Reading:

Habakkuk 2:4, Matthew 8, Galatians 3

*"Christ will always accept the faith that
puts its trust in Him."* –Andrew Murray

What's the difference between faith and hope? To be
sure, they are born from the same womb, but their
identities are uniquely distinct. The writer of
Hebrews said, "Now *faith* is the substance of things *hoped* for, the
evidence of things not seen" (Hebrews 11:1).

Hope speaks of our *desire*; faith speaks of our *dependence*.
Hope is a present comfort about a future event, whereas faith is a
present confidence in a promise or a person. When we hope for
something, we look toward the future with expectation. However,
when we demonstrate faith, we trust in a promise without having
proof or "the evidence of things not seen."

The minister of God needs *hope* so that he can press toward the
mark of the high calling, but he equally needs *faith* to take each
step, having not yet seen the finish line (but knowing it is there).
Faith is what substantiates our hope. John said, "For whatsoever is

born of God overcometh the world: and this is the victory that overcometh the world, *even our faith* (1 John 5:4).

- We are saved through *faith* (Ephesians 2:8)
- We are justified by *faith* (Romans 5:1)
- We are established in *faith* (Colossians 2:7)
- We work by *faith* (James 2:17)
- We walk by *faith* (2 Corinthians 5:7).
- Ultimately, we live by *faith* (Romans 1:17, Galatians 3:11)

Faith is not aimless; it is not blind. We have the "substance of things hoped for." And though there are things we have not seen, there is evidence to believe. "So then faith cometh by hearing, and hearing by the word of God" (Romans 10:17). Therefore, faith is our dependence, our trust, our reliance, our confidence in Christ. It is the "substance of things hoped for" validated, authenticated, and substantiated by the living Word of God.

It was faith that propelled every patriarch, prophet, and pilgrim into Hebrews 11. This same faith equips, inspires, and motivates every true minister of God today. It is faith that will one day rapture us into the presence of the One Who "dealt to every man a measure of faith." Then will our faith end in sight! What hope we have in faith!

TAKEAWAYS:

- Hope deals with desire; faith with dependence.
- Faith is established on the promises of God's Word.
- The ultimate reality of faith is being with Christ in heaven.

QUESTIONS:

Explain the difference between hope and faith.

_____

_____

_____

_____

_____

How does faith operate in your ministry?

_____

_____

_____

_____

_____

How can you grow in your faith? See I Peter 1:5-15.

_____

_____

_____

_____

_____

PRAYER:

Gracious Lord, It is by faith that I pray today. I believe in You, I trust in You, I rely upon the promises of Your Holy Word. Help me to walk and live by faith. Add to my faith all the virtuous qualities of Your kingdom. I long for the day when You will return, and my faith will end in sight.

66

SUFFICIENT GRACE

Selected Reading:

Genesis 6:1-8, Ruth 2:1-10, Titus 2:11-15

"Grace is but glory begun, and glory is
but glory perfected." –Jonathan Edwards

G race is the unmerited favor of God that reaches across
the chasm of our of depravity, quickens us with new
life and eternally declares us righteous before the
Father. The rich treasury of God's grace cannot be exhausted by
our sin debt. It abounds, it endures, it conquers, it saves, and it
suits every holy demand of heaven.

God has designed grace to be sufficient for every need of the
human experience. For the unregenerate there is saving grace. For
the weary soul there is sustaining grace. For the uncertain heart
there is secure grace. For the dying saint there is settled grace. For
all believers in all situations there is sufficient grace.

Author Jerry Bridges, in his book *The Disciplines of Grace*,
speaks of the all-encompassing power of grace at work in our
lives, "Your worst days are never so bad that you are beyond the
reach of God's grace. And your best days are never so good that

you are beyond the need of God's grace." What consolation there is to know that we are never beyond the reach, nor ever beyond the need of God's grace. Grace sustains us in every season of life and in every facet of ministry. To this truth, Paul could gladly testify.

Feeling the hurtful affliction of the thorn, and having "besought the Lord thrice," the apostle heard these comforting words of the Savior, "My grace is sufficient for thee: for my strength is made perfect in weakness" (2 Corinthians 12:9).

Grace is. Those are two wonderful words. It is comforting to look back and remember when "grace was." It is equally consoling to look ahead and trust that "grace shall be." But in the hour of despair, in the thorny briar patch of adversity, the balm needed for our desired healing lies in the fact that "grace *is* sufficient."

Written in the present perfect tense of the Greek, Paul was literally saying God's grace had been sufficient, God's grace will be sufficient, and God's grace presently was sufficient. For Paul, and for you and me, there is never a time, never a season, never a situation that depletes or drains the grace of God. With such a promise to claim, "Let us therefore come boldly unto the throne of grace, that we may obtain mercy, and find grace to help in time of need" (Hebrews 4:16).

TAKEAWAYS:

- Grace is not opposed to effort; it is opposed to earning.
- In every adverse situation there is a built-in infrastructure of divine grace.
- Grace enables us to draw nigh to God and find strength.

QUESTIONS:

How do you define "grace?" Give Scripture references.

_____

_____

_____

_____

_____

What does "sufficient grace" personally mean to you?

_____

_____

_____

_____

_____

How does grace work in the sanctification process of the believer?

_____

_____

_____

_____

_____

PRAYER:

Gracious Father, May I be reminded today that I not only need grace for salvation, I need grace for my struggle and trials. I need grace for the work of the ministry. I need grace for my own failures and sin. Grant Your grace in my time of need and let it be sufficient for the hour.

67

MERCY ANEW

Selected Reading:
Exodus 34:1-6, Joel 2:13, Hebrews 2:17

*"For I will be merciful unto their unrighteousness, and their sins
and their iniquities I will remember no more."* –Hebrews 8:12

I t is a constant outpouring. A perpetual stream that nourishes
the soul in continual fashion. It is available even now. Has
the day dawned? Have the birds yet eaten? Do you see the
shadows of the trees stretching across the sun-soaked field? Wipe
the sleep from your eyes and look out the window as far as you
can see or take a mere glance across the room. If it is a new day,
then mercy abides somewhere for the taking. This is the promise
of God.

To a generation that had bowed their knees to false gods,
turned their hearts from the temple, and experienced an exiled
existence in Babylon, Jeremiah, the weeping prophet declared:

"It is of the LORD's mercies that we are not consumed, because
his compassions fail not. They are new every morning: great is
thy faithfulness. The LORD is my portion, saith my soul;
therefore will I hope in him" (Lamentations 3:22-24).

At the start of every passing day, God supplies mercy anew. Why, may you ask, is there such a generous portion of divine restraint to saints and sinners? The answer is two-fold.

One, this is His nature, He is a merciful God. In His mercies, He spared Noah's family from the flood, preserved Lot from the fire, and delivered Israel from the plagues. David said, "He is ever merciful, and lendeth; and his seed is blessed" (Psalm 37:26). Furthermore, "The LORD is merciful, and gracious, slow to anger, and plenteous in mercy" (Psalm 103:8).

Two, His mercies are plenteous because we need mercy daily. In His grace, God imparts to us gifts that are undeserving such as hope, salvation, forgiveness, and heaven. However, in His mercy, He restrains from executing judgment against our sins and offers a way of escape from the condemnation that it brings. God offers mercy because He is faithful to do so, but He equally offers mercy because we desperately and daily need it.

Have you failed? There is mercy. Have you stumbled? There is mercy. Have you grown indifferent? There is mercy. Have you entangled your heart and mind with the affairs of this world? There is mercy. Have you awakened to this day only to find yourself in desperate need of restoration? Be of good cheer, once again, God has provided what the soul needs: Mercy anew.

TAKEAWAYS:

- There is a daily offering of mercy from God.
- Mercy is the restraint of God's judgment in my life.
- Mercy is richly given because God has it and I need it.

QUESTIONS:

Explain how mercy should never be used as an excuse for sin.

_____

_____

_____

_____

_____

How has the Lord demonstrated mercy to you in this very day?

_____

_____

_____

_____

_____

How has God's mercy influenced your relationship with others?

_____

_____

_____

_____

_____

PRAYER:

Wonderful, Merciful Savior, Great is Your name and greatly to be praised. I receive Your mercy today because I desperately need it. Wash me, forgive me, and hold back Your judgment against my life. Help me to extend the same mercies to those you do me wrong. Amen.

68

HOLY COMFORT

Selected Reading:
Luke 11:13, John 16:5-15, Ephesians 1:13,

"We must not suppose that the measure of our understanding or experience is the full measure of the Spirit's working." –John Murray

If there be any comfort or consolation to the spirit of man it can only be administered by the Spirit of God. As the wind "bloweth where it listeth," and cools the weary traveler from the noon-day sun, even so the Holy Comforter enraptures the soul and dispenses His divine solace to the troubled heart.

Such was the anxiety of the disciples in the upper room. Their last meal with the Master turned into a somber supper of sadness. The topics of discussion were betrayal, denial, and execution on a cross. The breaking of bread quickly turned into the breaking of hearts.

Jesus, knowing the angst of His apostles gave assurance of Another. Not another disciple, not another preacher, not another prophet, but Another Comforter, "And I will pray the Father, and he shall give you another Comforter, that he may abide with you forever;" (John 14:16). The power of the promised Spirit would be so magnanimous a gift that the departure of Christ would be considered an act of benevolence, "It is expedient for you that I go away: for if I go not away, the Comforter will not come unto you, but if I depart, I will send him unto you" (John 16:7).

The dynamic force of the Spirit not only breezed through their soul in the upper room, but inevitably rushed through their spirits as a mighty rushing wind on the day of Pentecost. Those hesitant, heart-broken disciples became fiery apostles who turned the world upside down. Speaking of the comfort of the Holy Spirit, John Owens wrote,

> "His work is to administer consolation unto believers, as being the only Comforter of the church. Now, he administers comfort no other way but by giving unto the minds and souls of believers a spiritual, sensible experience of the reality and power of the things we do believe. Other means of spiritual consolation I know none; and I'm sure this never fails."

Are you downtrodden and troubled in life and ministry? May I pose this question: Is it not the same Spirit that resides in you Who comforted the hearts of those original disciples? He ever lives to teach us, pray for us, guide us, and comfort us in all our troubles.

TAKEAWAYS:

- Only a regenerate believer can be filled with the Spirit.
- The work of the Spirit brings comfort by illuminating truth in God's Word and by pointing us to Christ.
- The Spirit's comfort enables and empowers us for the work of the ministry.

QUESTIONS:

List specific ways in which the Holy Spirit comforts His believers.

_____

_____

_____

_____

_____

Cite passages that describe the work of the Spirit of God.

_____

_____

_____

_____

_____

Is it possible for a believer to become "more" Spirit-filled?

_____

_____

_____

_____

_____

PRAYER:

Holy Spirit of God, When I cannot muster the words to pray, You groan on my behalf before the heavenly Father. I thank You for being a Comforter to me and in me. As You direct me to Christ and teach me the Word, I find great consolation in my soul. Lead me by Thy power!

69

LIBERATING TRUTH

Selected Reading:

1 Kings 2:1-4, Proverbs 23:23, Ephesians 6:14

*"Nothing gives rest like the sincere
search for truth."* –Blaise Pascal

In 1640, Puritan settlers printed the "Bay Psalm Book," a translation of the Old Testament psalms. Known as the first book printed in the United States of America, it recently sold at a Sotheby's auction as the most expensive book in the world. The bidding opened at $6 million and within a few moments closed at the astronomical price of $14.16 million. Some conclude that the winning buyer got a bargain; the book has an estimated value of over $20 million.

The truth is the contents therein cannot be measured in monetary terms. Solomon said the Word of God is more precious than gold or silver. The Bible is the only book in the world that offers hope to the hopeless, life to the dying, bread to the hungry, water to the thirsty, peace to the weary, and salvation to the sinner. The Bible is God's revelation of Himself to fallen humanity. It is the key that unlocks the chain to man's utter despair.

Just how valuable is the truth? Jesus said, "And ye shall know the truth, and the truth shall make you free" (John 8:32). What price can you put on soul liberty? How much would one pay for spiritual freedom? God's Word offers emancipation from sin, liberation from guilt, and deliverance from eternal hell.

"And ye shall know the truth" is a particularly important consideration when it comes to understanding the value of God's Word. Notice the phrasing of the Lord. He did not say "the truth shall make you free" but rather "the truth that you know" shall make you free. We will be hard-pressed to implement truth in our lives if we do not know what truth is. A.W. Tozer said, "The Word of God well understood and religiously obeyed is the shortest route to spiritual perfection. Nothing less than a whole Bible can make a whole Christian."

To be a "whole Christian" and to have a "whole ministry" one must dedicate their lives to the study and examination of truth. The minster of God who labors in word and doctrine is counted worthy of double honor. Not only does he have the distinct privilege of proclaiming the divine oracles of God, but he also knows the awesome power of being made free from the very Word He proclaims!

TAKEAWAYS:

- There is no limit to the value of God's Word.
- It is not the truth alone that makes us free, it is the truth that we know and apply.
- The minister who labors in truth is worthy of honor.

QUESTIONS:

Do you memorize Scripture on a regular basis? If so, how much?

_____

_____

_____

_____

_____

How would you distinguish "the truth" verses "the truth you know?"

_____

_____

_____

_____

_____

How does the Word of God console your heart as a minister?

_____

_____

_____

_____

_____

PRAYER:

Word of God, Speak that I may hear. Let me hear that I may obey. Let me obey so that men can see my good works and glorify the Father. Let the truth make me free; and in my freedom may others know the awesome-working power of Your deliverance and salvation. Amen!

70

DIVINE GLORY

Selected Reading:

Numbers 14:21, Isaiah 42:8, 2 Corinthians 3:18

"A dairy maid can milk cows
to the glory of God." –Martin Luther

There is no greater consolation in the work of God than to realize you exist for His glory. To this "chief end" we labor knowing that we were created and redeemed for His good pleasure. As the trophies of His grace, He will forever enjoy us as we forever enjoy Him. God delights in us, and His delight in us ought to bring the grandest elation of all. Thomas Manton, in his volume of *Works* succinctly said:

> "This life is not to be valued but as it yields opportunities to glorify God. We were not sent into the world to live for ourselves, but for God. If we could be our own first cause, then we might be our own end. But God made us for Himself and sent us into the world for Himself. It is not our duty to glorify God in heaven only, but also here on earth."

Paul said, "And whatsoever ye do in word or deed, do all in the name of the Lord Jesus, giving thanks to God and the Father by him" (Colossians 3:17). Furthermore, "Whether therefore ye eat, or drink, or whatsoever ye do, do all to the glory of God." (1 Corinthians 10:31). Jesus said of His own ministry, "I have glorified thee on the earth: I have finished the work which thou hast given me to do" (John 17:4). Such is the essence of glory.

The finished work of Christ provides a divine framework for the exaltation of God's glory in our lives. When we gladly and obediently fulfill His assignments for the express purpose of His honor, we are accomplishing His objective of making Him known to others. Jesus said, "And all mine are thine, and thine are mine; and I am glorified in them" (John 17:6,10). Christ glorified the Father, and the Father glorified Christ. However, those whom the Father gave to the Son glorified Christ in the world. This is our dutiful and delightful obligation until He returns. This is His glory.

One day, every knee will bow, and every tongue will confess that Jesus Christ is Lord, to the glory of God the Father. As much as it is our desire to *hear* the words "Well done," it is equally His desire to *say* them. His delight in us and our delight in Him will be joined together in celestial bliss. It will take all of eternity to discover and to enjoy the glory of our God, but such rapture can begin right here on earth as we faithfully labor for His honor.

TAKEAWAYS:

- The primary reason for man's existence is to glorify God.
- God delights in us as His trophies of grace.
- We glorify God on earth as gladly obey Him and faithfully make Him known to others.

QUESTIONS:

What passages in Jesus' ministry deals with the glory of God?

_____

_____

_____

_____

_____

List three ways in which you can glorify God in the earth:

_____

_____

_____

_____

_____

What consolation is there for the minister in the glory of God?

_____

_____

_____

_____

PRAYER:

Glorious Savior, Receive honor, and blessing, and power, and glory from my life. May I delight myself with obedient intention to Your good name. Find pleasure in me and help me fulfill every assignment so that others can know You and glorify Your name. Glorify Your name in the earth.

SUBJECT INDEX

AUTHOR INDEX

ABOUT THE AUTHOR

Kenneth Kuykendall has been the pastor of Cross Roads Baptist Church in Lawrenceville, Georgia since 2008. Under his leadership, the church has experienced spiritual growth, numerical increase, and facility expansion for years. His burden for ministry is to equip the saints, reach the unsaved with the gospel, and glorify Christ through expositional preaching and teaching.

In addition to the pastorate, he has written many books and Christian literature for ministry. In 2007, he started *Cross Roads Publications* which provides a variety of resources for churches, ministers, and individuals. He is also the founder of *Seeds for the Soul Daily Devotion*, a devotional ministry that reaches hundreds of thousands of subscribers.

He enjoys reading, praying, writing, hiking, running, and spending time with his family. He and his wife Heather have been married since 2000. They, along with their three sons, Brady, Drew, and Carson currently live in Loganville, GA.